scientific

SELF-DEFENSE

*A*s a youth, author A. P. Harrington went in for wrestling. Then—at 16—he discovered judo.

He joined the South London Judo Society and, in just 23 months, was awarded the coveted Black Belt . . . the youngest holder of that honor in Great Britain.

Since that time he has become one of the foremost teachers of judo . . . in the armed services, at London Polytechnic, and at the South London Judo Society. He is a member of the famous Budo-Kway.

Now, he draws on that experience to provide every boy with a careful, step-by-step guide to judo, the scientific art of self-defense.

*H*ere are all things you need to know . . . muscle-building exercises . . . five "secrets" of breaking a fall . . . hip throws, ankle throws, rear throws . . . complete with 87 pictures!

D1714534

Other SIGNET KEY Books You Will Enjoy
(50 cents each)

A. P. HARRINGTON
Black Belt 2nd Dan

EVERY BOY'S
JUDO

ILLUSTRATED BY
FRED THOMPSON

A SIGNET KEY BOOK

PUBLISHED BY THE NEW AMERICAN LIBRARY

Published as a SIGNET KEY BOOK by arrangement with Emerson Books, Inc., who have authorized this softcover edition. A hardcover edition is available from Emerson Books, Inc., at $2.95.

THIRD PRINTING

SIGNET TRADEMARK REG. U.S. PAT. OFF. AND FOREIGN COUNTRIES
REGISTERED TRADEMARK—MARCA REGISTRADA
HECHO EN CHICAGO, U.S.A.

SIGNET KEY BOOKS are published by
The New American Library, Inc.,
1301 Avenue of the Americas, New York, New York 10019

FIRST PRINTING, OCTOBER, 1966

PRINTED IN THE UNITED STATES OF AMERICA

ACKNOWLEDGEMENTS

I wish to thank my brother James for helping to demonstrate all the techniques used for illustrating this book.

I am also grateful to my friend Fred Thompson, Director of International Artists, for his artistic interpretation of the selected Judo movements which have been dealt with.

Further I would like to take this opportunity of offering my thanks to my instructors, past and present, and notably Mr. T. P. Leggett (6th Dan) of The Budokwai, whose ability as a teacher of the art of Judo is second to none.

Contents

Author's Introduction

I have devised this book for boys because I feel that the sport of Judo is ideally suitable for boys to learn. As a sporting activity it has much to offer: self-reliance, a fit body coupled with an alert mind, while encouraging the ability to make quick decisions.

I have not designed this book to cover every section of the art, but have set out to provide a reasonably stylish and effective form of Judo suitable for young men. In Japan many of the leading experts of the present day started practising the sport at a very early age, and I feel that there is no reason why youngsters of other countries cannot follow their example to good effect. A great advantage of starting Judo when young is that the muscles of the body have not had time to become too hard, and consequently one tends to adapt oneself more easily to the art. The thing for you to remember is that you have the greatest assets of all on your side—time and youth. For this reason there is no need to hurry through this book in an effort to master every technique as quickly as possible; and then find in the end that you have not attained a useful and clever style of Judo. It is far more worth while to be patient and to study each particular technique carefully, in order that you completely master the essentials and do not forget them, irrespective of the passage of time.

In an effort to make the technical explanations much easier to follow, I have segregated the movements for each technique before arranging them in sentences that follow the sequence of the action being described. In effect, what I have tried to do can be compared with the old-fashioned movie camera, where each picture was followed by another as the operator turned the handle. If you look at each sentence in the same way and then turn the handle, as it were, so that they all join together to become a complete movement, you will be able to picture each compound action more easily.

In the illustrations and text you will notice that most of the techniques can be reversed, so that you are able to perform them a different way round. For this purpose, I think that it would be a good idea for you to look at the illustrations in a mirror, in order that the action of the figures becomes reversed. You will then be able to picture the difference necessary in your posture.

When you are practising Judo you will need the assistance of a friend, a suitable mat, and an old jacket. Your friend should be your partner for the first two months, while you both study the technique together. Any mat composed of rubber, fibre or straw covered with a canvas will prove suitable (even old mattresses, covered with a canvas sheet, will also prove sufficient). In Judo clubs a jacket made of cotton material and fashioned after the style worn by coolies is used, together with three-quarter-length trousers, to give maximum freedom of movement. However, an extra large jacket of coarse texture will suffice, provided all the buttons are removed and the pocket flaps are sewn up. A sash tied round your waist is all that is required to stop the jacket from coming open at the front. To complete your outfit a pair of short trousers are needed. You should not wear shoes, because many throwing actions incorporate a sweeping action with a foot against an opponent's leg.

London   A. P. HARRINGTON

1/ PHYSICAL EXERCISES

THERE is a widespread notion that with the aid of a few Judo tricks a person can dispose of any opponent with a mere flick of the wrist. This idea is very misleading, inasmuch as it tends to give people the impression that Judo is a form of magic, instead of the hardworking sport that it is in reality.

Let us imagine that we are watching two Judo exponents, whom we will term as 'A' and 'B', engaged in a friendly practice. 'A' is a skilful, but physically small, Judo student, whereas 'B' is in the heavyweight class but does not possess so much skill. To weigh the assets of each man, I have prepared two tables to bear out a theory, in which the advantages of 'A' and 'B' are treated as terms of overall body weight:

'A'		'B'	
Body weight	98 pounds	Body weight	210 pounds
Skill and Speed of Movement	294 pounds	Skill and Speed of Movement	140 pounds
Strength	14 pounds	Strength	70 pounds
Total	406 pounds	Total	420 pounds

From this little experiment I think we can rightly conclude that 'B' would be in a stronger position, even considering the benefits of speed of movement and skill used by 'A'.

Now let us picture a further two men, whom we will term as 'C' and 'D', with 'C' being the lighter of the two men.

'C'		'D'	
Body weight	98 pounds	Body weight	210 pounds
Skill and Speed of Movement	294 pounds	Skill and Speed of Movement	140 pounds
Strength	42 pounds	Strength	70 pounds
Total	434 pounds	Total	420 pounds

From this alternative table it can be seen that the smaller of the two men has the advantage, by having a reasonable amount of strength at his command.

By this theory I do not intend to give you the idea that to be successful in Judo a person must develop his physique until he becomes 'muscle bound'. On the contrary, the whole purpose of exercising should be to make the body strong, yet supple. Exercises for the legs and lower body are given preference in the following nine examples, since I consider that Immobilization Holds, which are dealt with later, are sufficient in themselves for developing the strength of the upper body and for increasing stamina.

1st Exercise

Sit down on the mat with your legs stretched in front of you. Turning your body almost a half turn to the right, swing your bent right leg round in front of you, and rest the outside part of the same leg and foot on the surface. During this turning action your left foot ought not to leave the ground, it should merely be turned inwards, so that the inside of your left leg rests against the mat. Place the palm of your right hand on the surface close to the outside of your right thigh and position the palm of your

FIG. 1

left hand on the mat between the inside of your thighs (Fig. 1). Now raise your hands from the mat, then return them to their original positions, at the same time using them to push your body up in a springing action. During this movement the front part of your feet should not leave the mat. Once again push your body upwards even higher and return back to the same position as before. Now raise your body for the third time, but when you have lifted yourself as much as possible, twist your upper body to the left, and face your left foot by pivoting around on the toes of your feet. When you recline back to the mat this time, the outside part of your lower left leg contacts the mat in front of you, while your lower right leg is lowered in such a way that the inside part touches the surface behind you.

Once you are in the starting position, the exercise consists of gradually raising your body from the mat and, on the third time, twisting from the hips, so that you drop back to the mat in an entirely reversed position. You should repeat this activity several times in order that you face first one way and then the other.

2nd Exercise

To practice this exercise you will need the help of a friend. Lie down with your back on the mat and bend both legs, keeping your arms at right angles to your body. Ask your partner to stand facing you, then raise your feet from the floor, and with the toes pointing slightly outwards, place them against the front of his stomach. Your friend then gripping your ankles with his hands, should keep his feet, with toes pointing outwards, about one yard apart and incline his upper body forward.

Meanwhile you should ensure that the majority of his weight is comfortably supported on your feet. Continue your movements by very slowly bending your legs (Fig. 2). When your legs become well bent and your knee caps are pressing against your chest, slowly straighten your legs by pressing your feet firmly against the front of his stomach. Supporting the greater part of your partner's weight in this way you should slowly bend and straighten your legs some twenty times to gain the maximum benefit from this activity. After your partner has assisted you, give him the opportunity of practising the exercise by changing positions with him.

FIG. 2

3rd Exercise
This exercise is somewhat harder on the leg muscles than the previous one and if you find it too hard you should diligently practise the easier one. You will once again need the help of a friend.

Stand facing your partner, then turn to your left so that your right side is nearest to him. Grip the inside of his right upper jacket sleeve with your left hand, then place your right foot in between his feet, bending both legs as you do so. With your left hand, which should still be gripping his sleeve, pull his right arm behind your head, and at the same time thrust your right hand between his legs and grasp the back of his right thigh. These movements will cause him to lean forward and be supported on your upper back. Raise him from the mat by continuing to pull at his right sleeve with your left hand and straightening your legs. Support your friend steadily across your shoulders by planting your feet on the mat shoulder width apart (Fig. 3). The final stage of the exercise is to bend and straighten your legs, while supporting the total weight of your partner. Do not repeat the knee bends too many times until you have practised the exercise on a number of separate occasions.

FIG. 3

4th Exercise

Stand facing your partner, with your feet about shoulder width apart, and grip the outside of his right upper jacket sleeve with your left hand. Move your right leg forward in front of your left leg, placing the ball of your right foot on the mat just by the inside of his right foot. Turn your body round to the left by pivoting on the ball of your right foot, until you are facing the same direction as your partner, then well bend both of your legs. After this turn is completed place your left foot on the mat close

FIG. 4

FIG. 5

by the inside of his left foot and pass your right arm
around his waist. Tighten your hold on your partner's
waist and pull his right sleeve forward to your left with
your left hand, in order that his stomach presses firmly
against your lower back. Ensure that you have a good
sense of balance by keeping your toes pointing slightly
outwards, then partially straighten your legs to lift your
partner clear of the mat (Fig. 4). Still supporting your
friend on the right side of your lower back, bend and
straighten your legs five times.

5th Exercise

Keeping your feet about shoulder width apart, stand with
your back against your partner's and link your arms
through his. Bend your legs and clench your fists in front
of your hips, in order to secure a firm hold on his upper
arms. When you achieve this grip bend forward from the
waist so that your partner is drawn on to your back.
Straighten your legs to such an extent that you lift him
from the ground (Fig. 5).

For you to get the utmost benefit from this exercise
your friend should allow his legs to hang limply, to make
himself become a 'dead weight'. Straighten your legs and
also unbend your body from the waist upwards, until you
have put your partner back on his feet. He should make
sure that he brings his feet to the mat shoulder width
apart, because from this stance he will be in a position to
reverse his former part in the exercise and lift you from
the ground. Repeat this exercise for some five minutes,
in the course of which you should lift one another many
times.

6th Exercise

'Press-ups' are a very well known form of exercise. This
particular method is a variation of them, especially devised for strengthening the fingers quite apart from the
arm muscles.

Lie face downwards on the mat keeping your legs
close together. Spread your fingers, then place the tips of
your fingers and thumbs on the floor in such a way that
your hands are directly below your shoulders. Now slowly

raise your body from the mat by straightening your arms, until you are supporting your body on the tips of your fingers, thumbs, and toes (Fig. 6). Partially bend your arms and lower yourself, without allowing your body to touch the ground. Repeat this whole movement five times, before you once again relax back into the starting position. It is most important for you to breathe correctly, which, in this instance, is to inhale as you straighten your arms and exhale when you bend them.

7th Exercise

Lie down with your back resting on the mat, then raise your legs from the surface and fully bend them. Tensing your calf muscles, powerfully straighten your right leg

and imagine that you are kicking with your heel (Fig. 7). Immediately that you have performed this kicking action, bend your right leg and repeat the same kicking action with your left leg.

Continue alternately kicking, first with your right and then with your left leg, for about five minutes. You should be careful to see that your legs do not follow a cycling motion, instead of performing vigorous kicking actions.

8th Exercise

Apart from being a useful activity for strengthening the legs, this exercise is ideal for getting used to supporting the weight of your body on one leg.

Stand with your feet about twenty-four inches apart with the toes pointing outwards. Fully bending your right leg, incline your upper body over to your right until your head is close to your right knee. Transfer all the weight of your body on to your bent right leg and slide your left leg outwards to the left until you are able to rest the inside edge of your foot and lower left leg on the mat (Fig. 8).

Regain your original starting position, then fully bend your left leg and incline your upper body over to your left until your head is positioned close to your left knee. Once this action is accomplished slide your right foot outwards to the right, so that the inside edge of your right foot and lower right leg rest against the mat.

FIG. 6

FIG. 7

Carry out these actions for five minutes and make sure that your balance remains stable thoughout the change of your position.

FIG. 8

9th Exercise

Begin this exercise by crouching down on the mat. Slightly bending your arms, place the palms of your hands on the ground directly below your shoulders. Support the weight of your body with your hands and left foot, then straighten your right leg by sliding your right foot backwards along the surface. Raise your straight right leg from the mat, and keeping it parallel to the ground swing it in an anti-clockwise direction towards your front. In order to allow it to pass comfortably underneath your right arm, quickly raise your right hand about twelve inches from the mat. Speedily replace your right hand to its original position, and without stopping the circular movement of your right leg, raise your left hand from the surface (Fig. 9). When your right leg has passed underneath your left arm, return your left hand to the mat and do a little hop with your left foot, so that you can bring your right leg to complete a full circle, by passing it underneath your left leg.

You should now be in the same position that you were in at the start of the exercise. Only pause for a moment at the completion of the movement, before once again starting to swing your right leg round in an anti-clockwise direction. Your aim should be to practise this activ-

ity until you are able to describe five complete and con-
secutive circles with your right leg. When you become
competent at swinging your right leg round, reverse the
instructions where necessary in order that you swing
your left leg round in a clock-wise direction.

FIG. 9

2/ HOW TO BREAK A FALL

(UKEMI)

THE way of learning how to break a fall is the most important thing for anyone to know when practising Judo. No matter how efficient you become with the other sections of the art it will be of little value if you cannot make a safe recovery from each and every fall. For this reason it is a general custom in Judo clubs for all members to practise the various methods of breaking a fall at the beginning and end of every session of Judo. Under no circumstances should you skimp over this section of the book, and I advise you to spare no effort in perfecting the art of falling before you even look at the throwing techniques.

The general rules to bear in mind when breaking a fall are: to keep relaxed, roll to the ground in the shape of a wheel, keeping your head and joints tucked out of harm's way, reduce the force and absorb the shock of the fall by striking the ground with your arms or legs.

In most sports, take for example football, it is usually enough for a player to curl up his body and keep his head and joints protected should he fall. I must make it quite clear to you that in the sport of Judo these precautions would not be sufficient in themselves. The main drawback is that when practising Judo you would not merely be called upon to sustain the shock of an unintentional fall, but you are, more often than not, likely to be thrown on to the mat by an opponent with considerable vigour. To compensate for the disadvantage of your being thrown at such speed, your partner must always put you down to the mat squarely on to your back and retain a grip on your jacket with one hand. The reason why you must be guided to the mat in this way is so that you will be in a favourable position to use your arms to break the fall. By striking the mat with an arm, the shock of a fall sustained by your body is negligible; it has been calculated that the beat absorbs 95 per cent of the shock.

When using your arms to absorb the shock of a fall, make sure that they are kept relaxed. To illustrate this point further, I am going to give a comparison. Most of us at one time or another have visited the circus and enjoyed the sight of an animal trainer's skilful use of a long whip. When the thong lashes the ground it appears to be rigid. To get this effect the trainer has mastered the art of swishing the flexible lash through the air at great speed, so that as it strikes the ground it becomes taut. Liken yourself to the trainer and imagine your arm to be his whip, with which you can strike the mat in the same way, in order that it also appears rigid.

1st Method

Lie down with your back resting on the mat, then bend both of your legs and place the soles of your feet on the ground. Keep your chin tucked on to your chest and raise your arms in front of your face, crossing them at the wrists with the palms away from you (Fig. 10). Allow your arms to flop down and gently slap the mat, with the palms of your hands about ten inches from the sides of your body, while ascertaining that you strike the mat with the underside part of your arms, from the tips of your fingers to your armpits.

Practise these movements for five minutes and relax the muscles of your arms each time after striking the mat.

Without using any force to beat the mat at first, develop an easy rhythmic movement with both arms. When you have achieved this rhythm gradually increase the power and speed of your arm actions, and make a fairly loud noise each time that you slap the canvas.

2nd Method

Sit down on the mat with your legs outstretched and close together. Bend your right arm and bring it across your body in such a way that you are able to place the palm of your right hand on your left shoulder. Tuck your chin on to your chest, then lower your back to the ground and

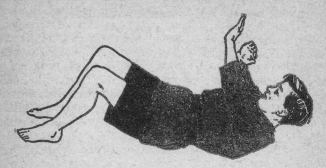

FIG. 10

FIG. 11

as you do so beat the mat ten inches from your right side with the palm of your right hand (Fig. 11). When your right arm contacts the mat bring your legs into the air, until the base of your spine is clear of the mat. Once again return to the sitting position. Now bend your left arm, placing the palm of your left hand on your right shoulder and lower your back to the ground, this time striking the mat with your left arm. Return to the sitting position. This action performed by your body is similar to that which is effected by the rocker on the bottom of a baby's rocking-horse.

You should repeat this method of breaking a fall by using each arm alternately for some fifteen minutes, and as you progress hit the mat with more effort. The important object to achieve is to beat the mat a split second before your shoulder-blades contact the surface, consequently do not continue until you have mastered this timing.

3rd Method

Lie face downwards on the mat with your legs and feet pressed closely together. Lift your body from the ground by placing the palms of your hands against the surface directly below your shoulders and then straightening your arms. Raise your left hand from the mat and take back your left side to such a degree that your right side is brought nearest the ground and your body is supported on your straight right arm and outside part of your right foot. Fully extend your left arm above your left shoulder and tuck your chin on to your chest (Fig. 12). Your body at this stage should almost conform to the letter T when viewed from the side. Slightly bend your left arm and by slowly lowering it pass it underneath your stomach. As soon as your left hand begins to pass slowly underneath your stomach, allow your body to follow the turning action of your arm by twisting your hips to the right. These turning movements will cause your body to spin in the way that a miniature globe of the earth will revolve round its rod, and the impetus of the turn will push your right hand outwards in front of you.

You must break the mild fall by using your right arm to strike the mat close to your right side, just before

FIG. 12

your back touches the surface. Practise this twisting
movement of your body in slow motion, until you can
judge the correct moment when to thump the mat with
your right arm. After you have diligently practised this
method of breaking a fall many times you should gradually increase the speed of your movements, until you spin
yourself over on to your back with the utmost speed. If
you practise this turn with perseverance there is no
chance of ever being thrown at a faster pace, so you will
never be in a position when you are not able to break
a fall. Most men in Judo use 'right-handed' throwing actions which necessitate their opponent's breaking the fall
with their left arm when they are thrown. For this reason
you must also practise breaking the fall with your left
arm by reversing the instructions where necessary.

4th Method
For practising this type of falling activity you will need
the assistance of a partner. You should begin by standing
with your right side nearest to him. Grip his left jacket

lapel with your right hand and request him to grip your
right jacket sleeve with his left hand. Your friend should
keep his feet about shoulder width apart and his legs
slightly bent. Now bend your left arm and place the palm
of your left hand on the front of your right shoulder. To
continue your movements slide your left foot forward
along the mat and fully bend your right leg. In order that
you keep your balance for as long as possible curve your
upper body forward and tuck your chin on to your chest.
These movements will cause you to lose your balance and
roll backwards to the ground. You should break the gentle

FIG. 13

fall by striking the mat with your left arm (Fig. 13). Just after you have broken the fall in this way, raise your legs so that the bottom of your spine is clear of the mat at the completion of your continuous rolling movement. To regain your starting position simply roll forward and stand up. Your partner must maintain his hold on your right jacket sleeve throughout this activity, and make his balance secure by bending his legs, keeping his upper body straight and holding his head back. He should also pull at your jacket sleeve as you lose balance in order that he is in a position to slow down the speed of your falls. After you have practised breaking the fall in slow motion many times, steadily increase the speed of your movements until you reach the stage where it is possible for you to jump into the air to such a degree that you fall at the utmost speed. When you are quite confident of breaking the fall by using your left arm reverse the instructions where necessary, so that you use your right arm to absorb the shock of the falls.

Once you have become used to breaking the fall with either arm, change places with your partner and offer him the opportunity of practising this method of breaking a fall.

5th Method
From a standing position well bend your right leg, place the palms of your hands on the mat directly below your

FIG. 14

shoulders, and by sliding on the toes of your left foot
stretch your left leg behind you. Raise your right hand
from the mat and position it between your chest and the
ground, so that your fingers point towards your left foot,
with the thumb of your hand kept uppermost. See that
your slightly curved right arm is kept rigid and that the
fingers of your right hand are pressed closely together.
Keeping your chin tucked well on to your left collar-bone,
bring the little finger edge of your right hand against the
mat (Fig. 14). Begin to roll **slowly** forward contacting
the mat in turn with the outside of your right forearm,
then your right upper arm, and as you turn head over
heels your right shoulder-blade. Just before your lower
back touches the mat break the fall with your left arm,
absorbing part of the shock by bringing your right foot
over your slightly bent left leg and stamping the sole of
the foot against the mat (Fig. 15).

Carry out this complete movement many times in slow
motion, without trying to speed up your actions. When
you have perfected the timing of the movement gradually increase the speed of your forward roll so that you
beat the mat with considerable power. On no account
should you attempt the rolling movements at great speed,
by running forward, until you are absolutely certain of
your ability to perform them correctly. Once you have

FIG. 15

mastered the forward roll by using your right arm, reverse the instructions and use your left arm as a support for your body as you turn head over heels; but
remember to start with the primary stage at first.

IT IS essential that you learn to move about the mat correctly before you start practising throwing techniques with a partner. Your aim should be to try for a style of Judo that relies on quick and fluid movements. I think it very worthwhile for you to always spend five minutes at the beginning and end of every practice session to the improvement of your general movement.

Begin by standing with your feet about shoulder width apart and your toes turned slightly outwards. Step a small pace sideways with your left foot, followed by an equal pace in the same direction with your right foot. At no point should your feet be brought too close together as it will make it easier for an opponent to break your balance later on. On the other hand, if your feet are kept too far apart and your legs as well bent your balance may be difficult to disturb, but your speed of movement is considerably reduced. When you move around the mat purposely wriggle your upper body about to keep it relaxed and supple. Practise these movements for a few minutes then reverse the actions of your feet by moving in an anti-clockwise direction round the mat. Do this by stepping a small pace sideways with your right foot followed by a similar pace with your left foot. Take care that you do not drag your left foot behind your right foot instead of making a separate step.

Do not stare down at your feet while moving about the mat, but glance around at your surroundings in a line with your shoulders. After you become adept at circling the mat, both to your left and to the right, move freely about the mat in any direction you wish, but remember to apply the same basic rules of posture and feet movements. When you have mastered this way of moving you will pave the way for developing a good style of Judo. Unless you try hard to perfect this style, you will tend to pick up faults in your posture, which you will find very hard to correct at a later stage in your training.

Now it will be necessary for you to have the help of a partner. Stand facing each other, then take hold of each other's left jacket lapel with the right hand and with the left hand grasp each other's right jacket sleeve close to the elbow (Fig. 16). Both of you should keep your arms slightly bent and take your grips very lightly, in order that your arm muscles do not become tensed and slow down the rapidity of your movements. Move about the mat together for about ten minutes and slide the soles of your feet along the ground, keeping your toes pointing slightly outwards. Although your heels ought to be kept on the ground, the weight of your body should be poised over the balls of your feet.

It was pointed out in the chapter on Physical Exercises that speed of movement plays a very important role in Judo. However, speed is not enough unless it is coupled with skill. Consequently let us consider an observation that I have made while teaching Judo which seems to explain very clearly what I mean.

If an action is made helter-skelter without proper thought because a person is nervous it is likely to be the wrong move for the situation. The ideal thing in Judo is to keep a calm but nevertheless receptive frame of

FIG. 16

mind, so that when a move is made against you, you will be able to use the right counter move more effectively. Let us consider this theory in a practical way.

Imagine yourself to be very frightened, by tensing all the muscles of your body, while thinking about a frightening experience, then make a right-handed punch with as much speed and power as you are able to muster. Now relax the muscles of your body and dismiss the fear from your mind and once again make a right-handed punch with your utmost speed and power.

You will notice that the second punching action you made was by far the more powerful and speedier of the two. This was because the complete and combined power of your mind and body was directed behind the blow. In the first punching action not only did you have to concentrate on making the blow, but most of your energies were wasted on keeping yourself in a tensed state.

A further example is that of an unfortunate artiste who appears on a stage in such a nervous state, that she is unable to speak—let alone move. This state of mind is commonly known as stage fright.

In this connection, a second point for you to note is that when you make a powerful movement, you should tense your stomach muscles and so draw extra power from them. Not only is your stomach region the focal point of your body's balance, I also think it is the centre of your body's strength. It is a natural reaction for the muscles of your body to become tensed when they have been used to bring about a violent action, consequently they should always be kept relaxed until a particular movement is about to be put into effect.

You should make up your mind from the beginning that throughout your study of Judo you will be thrown many times, and you must look upon it as part of your training. It is wrong to have a defensive attitude, because this will hinder your progress. Unfortunately some beginners fall into the bad habit of bending their legs and keeping their feet as far away from their opponent as possible. By using this 'crab-like' style they may succeed in causing a stalemate, but at a later stage in their training their defensive outlook will result in their being unable to score against inexperienced opponents.

4 / BREAKING AN OPPONENT'S BALANCE

(KUZUSHI)

THE key that opens the door to the mastery of Judo is the art of breaking an opponent's balance without resorting to force. A strong heavy man may find it fairly easy to lift bodily an average-sized man without skill. Although there is not much chance of the smaller man being able to lift the heavier man above his head, if he knows how to break his opponent's balance he will achieve the same result far more quickly, and with far less effort. I think that the Cornish-born Bob Fitzsimmons, one time Heavyweight Boxing Champion of the World, summed this principle up excellently (although in a different context) when he said, 'The bigger they come the heavier they fall.'

Here are three basic ways of breaking an opponent's balance. Each system will prove worthwhile so you should study each one carefully. Do not worry too much about the finer details, as these are explained in every throwing technique which we shall go into later.

1st System
This method of breaking an opponent's balance depends on your preventing his lower body from moving, by blocking his way with either your leg or foot. Ask your partner to stand facing you then grip his jacket in the region of his chest. Now place your right leg behind your partner's right leg and use your hands to tilt him over backwards to such a degree that he trips over your leg and falls backwards to the mat. You must, of course, only use gentle movements to safeguard him from any knocks; or alternatively he can break the mild fall by using his left arm.

To give you an example for this technique, I would like you to imagine a person stepping backwards for some reason, when his feet are trapped by an unnoticed obstacle, which causes him to pitch backwards and fall down on the ground. Although I have only given one specific direction when outlining the idea behind this particular method of breaking an opponent's balance, you can, of course, use the same method to any direction you wish. After you have gained a reasonable knowledge of the essentials change places with your partner so that he may practise.

2nd System

The idea behind this method of breaking an opponent's balance is to increase the length of his step to such an extent that he is unable to keep an upright posture and consequently falls over.

Stand by your partner's left side and grip his left sleeve close to the elbow joint with your right hand. Now ask him to step slowly forward with his left leg, and just before he places his left foot on the mat bring the sole of your right foot slowly forward against the back of his left ankle. When this movement causes him to over-step, make his balance become even more insecure by pulling his left sleeve downwards with your right hand. These actions will cause him to fall down and he should break the fall with his right arm. Once again you should vary your position so that you disturb his balance to other directions.

To illustrate the basic idea behind this second system, let us take as an example the scene pictured in so many comedy films. A man is walking along the pavement, bliss-fully unaware that a banana skin is lying in his path. When he steps on it his foot slips along the ground and he is caught completely by surprise as he is thrown off balance to the ground.

3rd System

In this method I will try to show you how important it is to recognize a habit and use it to your own advantage. For example, it is a natural instinct for a normal person to resist force of any shape or kind. Without taking an unfair advantage of your friend, make a little test to prove this point. Stand facing your friend and lightly grip his jacket lapels with your hands. Gently draw him towards you, and as you feel him resisting this pull by leaning backwards suddenly change your actions by stepping forward and pushing against the front of his chest. Instead of giving way to force, your friend will, I think, instinctively draw away from you and put himself off balance, making you the master of the situation. Again you will be able to vary your movements and accordingly make his balance insecure to other directions.

It will be clear to you that it is a good policy in Judo to always deflect rather than try to stop undue pressure of any kind. To expand this idea a little further, let us form a mental picture of a man holding a door against a gang of men, who are trying to push it open. If the defender suddenly gives way by opening the door and stepping aside, the crowd will pile up on the floor.

5 / GRADES AND CONTEST RULES OF JUDO

Grades of Judo

THROUGHOUT the world the measure of skill which a Judo exponent has attained is shown by the colour of the sash worn about the waist. While the black-belt grades are uniform in every country where Judo is practised, there are a few minor differences in the classification of the coloured belts worn in the Kyu (student) grades.

In the Unites States the following categories are used:

Beginner. 6th class (White Belt)
           5th class (White Belt)
           4th class (Green Belt)
           3rd class (Brown Belt)
           2nd class (Brown Belt)
           1st class (Brown Belt)

           1st Dan—10th Dan (Black Belt)

It is usual for the best 'contest men' to be found between the black-belt grades of 4th Dan and 6th Dan. For instance, the 1960 East-West Judo meet of Japan was won by Mr. Iwata, a young 4th Dan who weighs around 150 pounds.

Contest Rules of Judo
1. A contest shall begin after the ceremonial bow, and when the opponents have assumed a standing position, and shall last for five minutes, or until one of the contestants scores two points.
2. The winner of the contest shall be the individual who first scores two points or he who gets the only point, except as provided for otherwise in Rule 16. In the event of no points or equal points having been scored at the end of a specified period, the

Umpire may award the contest to the individual showing the best style or spirit, or he may pronounce the contest a draw.

3. A throw, a lock, and a hold shall each count one point.

4 A throw to be counted as a point must fulfil the following conditions:
   (a) It must be executed intentionally.
   (b) It must be executed with a certain impetus.
   (c) The opponent must be thrown on his back.

5. Should a contestant have been thrown according to Rule 4, it matters not how cleverly or quickly he changes his position afterwards and so throws his opponent; the first thrower gains the point, not the second.

6. When a competitor in a standing position cleverly lifts his opponent shoulder high, in such a way that a dangerous throw could be executed, the Umpire shall stop the throw and award him a point.

7. A throw shall be recognized even though a contestant falls outside the mat area if the fall be in accordance with Rules 4 and 8.

8. Any technique which is applied outside the mat area shall not be recognized.

9. Groundwork begins when a throw has been unsuccessful and one or both contestants fall to the ground. A contestant may not remain on the ground when his opponent is standing up and waiting.

10. Should one contestant go to the ground other than through the intended employment of a throwing technique, the Umpire may award a penalty point against him.

11. The following conditions are necessary for locks to be recognized:
    (a) The signal of defeat must be given by one competitor; or
    (b) the effect must be recognized by the Umpire.

12. When a contestant admits his defeat under a lock he shall call out or lightly tap the opponent or himself or the mat twice with his hand or foot.

13. A hold is counted as a point when a contestant

holds his opponent with his back wholly or largely
on the ground with one or more limbs under control for thirty seconds without a lock. The hold
is considered to be broken when an opponent puts
his arm or leg on the body of the holder in such
a way that a lock or a disturbance of the hold
may occur. The counting of the time for holding
shall not be interrupted by the termination of the
specified period for the contest.

14. When the contestants are locked on the ground so
that in the opinion of the Umpire neither contestant can extricate himself or gain any advantage over the other, the Umpire may order both
contestants to resume standing position.

15. The following actions are barred:
   (a) Throwing the opponent on his head, neck or
       shoulders.
   (b) Twisting or bending fingers, wrists, toes, jaw,
       head or spine.
   (c) Ankle locks, leg locks, kidney squeeze, pinch-
       ing or nerve pressing, blows.
   (d) Applying or pressing the hands against the
       opponent's face.
   (e) Pulling down the opponent for the purpose
       of beginning groundwork.
   (f) Squeezing the head with legs or arms.
   (g) Applying locks with a jerk.
   (h) Side Body Throws where either contestant is
       below 1st Kyu grade.
   (i) Gripping inside the openings of the sleeves or
       trousers.

16. Should a contestant infringe any of these Rules, the
Umpire may stop the contest and, without regard
to the score, decide the contest against the de-
faulter.

17. In all cases the decision of the Umpire (or Umpires)
shall be final.

6 / COMBINATION TECHNIQUES

(RENRAKU-WAZA)

THERE are two basic attacking methods of throwing an opponent. One is based on the idea of using a specific throwing action against him with the aim of putting the maximum amount of power and speed into the movement, in hope that it will cause him to be thrown. Although this system is widely used, when it fails it means that the attacker must revert to his starting position. An alternative method that is, in my opinion, by far the better of the two is based on the use of Combination Throws. This means that when an attempted throwing action has failed you will be able to try a different throw from another angle without a pause. For instance, if you have tried to throw your opponent in a forward direction and he has succeeded in blocking your movements by leaning backwards, it means that little resistance would be offered by him should you suddenly change the direction of your attack and throw him backwards. Provided you keep your body fairly supple when moving in for a throwing technique, you will find it possible to vary your movements immediately that you feel, or sense, that excessive resistance is forthcoming from an opponent.

Although I have selected certain throwing movements from Judo which lend themselves to be joined with others in combination attacks, I stress the fact that each and every one is a recognized technique which may be used by itself. After you have practised the collective methods of throwing actions, I recommend you to study the section devoted to Approach for Throwing Actions, on page 102, so that you are able to use the throwing techniques either in combination with one another or as separate attacking movements. Further, the section dealing with Obtaining Grips on an Opponent's Jacket on page 106 is most useful to know because it allows you to use a varied style of attack.

Group One

Inner Ankle Throws **(Ouchi-Gari)** and Shoulder Throws **(Seoinage)**

Inner Ankle Throw (1st method) **(Ouchi-Gari)**
Stand facing your partner with your feet about shoulder width apart and the toes pointing slightly outwards. Hold his right jacket sleeve close to the elbow joint with your left hand and use your right hand to grasp his left jacket lapel. Ask your partner to obtain grips on your jacket in a similar way, by grasping your right sleeve at the elbow with his left hand, while taking hold of your left lapel with his right hand. As soon as your partner has grasped your jacket, maintain your hold on his clothing and begin to tilt his upper body towards you. When he opposes the pulling action of your hands by bending his legs and leaning backwards, still continue to pull at his jacket so that he is forced to resist with even more effort. Step forward with your right foot and place it between his feet, then quickly bring your left foot forward, placing it just behind your right heel with the toes turned outwards. Slightly bend your left leg and support the weight of your body on it, in order that you can lift your right foot from between his feet and press the back of your right calf against the back of his left calf. At the completion of these movements the right side of your body should be nearest to him. Change the pulling motion of your right hand into a downward pushing one towards his right heel and then forward as you bend him over backwards (Fig. 17). Use your right lower leg to hook his left lower leg forward, compelling him to fall backwards. Just before his back touches the mat he ought to break the fall by striking the surface with his left arm.

When you begin to study a throwing technique use just enough speed and power to disturb your partner's balance, but stop immediately you feel he is about to fall. It is very boring for your partner if he is continuously thrown to the mat; apart from this the amount of time used by him in regaining his feet could be used by you for extra practice of the throwing movement. For these reasons you should carry out the movements leading up to the final throwing action many times without causing your partner to fall. After you have practised the movements, change roles with your partner so that he may try the technique against you.

The more you help one another in the early stages of your training, the more benefit you will derive later on. Moreover, if you are not concerned with having to worry

FIG. 17

about competition from your partner, you can convert the theory into practice much more easily. You cannot expect to master this or any other Judo technique in a matter of minutes, but if you practise diligently and spare no effort, you must win through in the end. The moral here is the same as in the story of Robert the Bruce and the spider—'If at first you don't succeed try, try, try again.'

It is most important that you do not waste time and effort needlessly by shuffling your feet about between each repetition of a throwing movement. For instance, in this variation of the Inner Ankle Throw, you begin by facing your partner, advancing your right foot and following it quickly with your left foot. You then raise your right foot from the mat in order that your lower right leg can be lodged behind his lower left leg. (In contests the natural conclusion would be for you to throw your opponent to the mat. Since we are only interested at the moment, however, in perfecting the movements that could result in a throw you must learn how to regain your starting position without loss of time.) Replace your right foot upon the mat and step a pace backwards with your left foot, then follow this by bringing your right foot backwards without allowing it to touch the mat, and as it nears your left foot bring it forward and start another throwing action. By this method of repeatedly doing an exact movement in slow motion, you will find it fairly easy to learn a technique, and speed up your actions as you make progress.

Shoulder Throw (1st method) (Seoinage)

This Shoulder Throw can be used in combination with the Inner Ankle Throw that I have just described. It is most usefully employed against a taller opponent who may have succeeded in avoiding your attempted Inner Ankle Throw by taking a large pace backwards with his left foot. In order that you will be ready to meet such a situation, ask your partner to evade your intended Inner Ankle Throw by stepping backwards with his left foot. To counter this move place the ball of your right foot upon the mat just inside his right foot, then slightly bend both legs. To make his balance insecure use the grips that you have maintained on his jacket to tilt his upper body forward in such a way that the majority of his weight is brought over the toes of his right foot. Pivoting round to your left on the ball of your right foot, continue to pull his right arm forward and slightly upwards with your

left hand. When you have almost turned to face the same
direction as your partner, bring your left foot backwards and place it on to the mat just inside his left foot.
Whilst you are making these movements with your
feet, you should twist your fully bent right arm inwards
and tuck your right elbow underneath his right armpit.
Take great care to keep the muscles of your right arm relaxed and also ensure that your right forearm is parallel
to the ground, with your right thumb pressing against the
front of your right shoulder. Now that you are positioned
directly in front of your partner, well bend your legs
and use your hands to draw him close to you. Your hips
should be below the line of his hips and your right buttock

FIG. 18

should be pressing against the front of his right thigh in
order to frustrate any attempt he might make to step
forward with his right leg. Most of the weight of your body
should be supported on your bent left leg (Fig. 18). Still

continuing to pull strongly at your partner's right jacket sleeve with your left hand, straighten your legs, then twist your hips slightly to the left and thrust your buttocks against the lower part of his stomach. As soon as your partner falls over your right hip, make sure that you release your grip on his left lapel and glide him safely down to the mat on his back (Fig. 19). He must break the fall by beating the mat strongly with his left arm and you can help to slow down his momentum by retaining your grip on his right jacket sleeve with your left hand.

In learning this throwing movement you will have to practise it many times and so, as I pointed out earlier, it is not advisable for you to throw your partner at each attempt.

FIG. 19

An essential feature of this technique is the importance of bending your legs sufficiently to get your hips well below the line of your partner's hips. The general feeling amongst the Japanese who practise Judo is that the average Occidental followers of the art do not bend their legs nearly enough where required, when attempting to throw an opponent. When I had the privilege of studying under T. Kawamura (Black Belt 7th Dan), a former Judo Champion of Japan, I was often amazed to see how much he lowered his body when throwing an opponent, in spite of the fact that he was six feet in height. The advantage of keeping to this rule is that you can 'down' an opponent with skill, rather than by burning up your energies in a trial of strength.

Inner Ankle Throw (2nd method) **(Ouchi-Gari)**
This alternative way of accomplishing the Inner Ankle Throw is very suitable for use against a much taller opponent, who may use a defensive crouch by keeping his legs well bent. Another time when you can use this method to your advantage is when an opponent is in the habit of turning his right side nearest to you, while keeping his right foot well in front of his left foot. Ask your partner to stand in this position with his right leg forward in order that you can practise this method of the Inner Ankle Throw.

Obtain the basic sleeve and lapel grip on one another's jacket. Tightening the hold that you have on your partner's jacket, pull him towards you. Invite him to resist this pull by in turn pulling at your jacket and leaning backwards (as he would probably do in reality). Step forward with your right foot and place it on the mat just inside the toes of his right foot. Now bring your left foot forward and position it on the mat close to the heel of your right foot. At the time that you make these movements with your feet release the grip that you have on his left jacket lapel, in order to bring your right hand downwards and press the little finger edge of your hand against the outside of his right thigh. Jerk his right sleeve downwards towards his right heel and place the weight of your body on your bent left leg. Now pass your right foot between his legs and lodge your lower right leg behind

the calf of his right leg. Bring your right shoulder against
the right side of his chest, continuing to press the outside edge of your lower right arm against the outside of
his right thigh, as you drive your right hand down towards
the mat. Your partner's posture should now be very insecure, and to destroy his balance completely hook your
right lower leg around his right calf and scoop his right
leg forward (Fig. 20). As soon as your partner falls over
backwards to the mat, he must keep his chin tucked on
to his chest and break the fall by striking the mat with
his left arm.

It is essential for you to keep pulling at your partner's
right jacket sleeve for as long as possible in this technique. This will enforce your partner to concentrate on
resisting your pull and consequently allow you to use
his forceful opposition to your own advantage. Once
again remember that it is not expedient to throw one
another too many times whilst practising.

It is perhaps worthy of note that this type of throwing
action can be most useful should you be engaged in a
contest against an opponent whose exact measure of skill
is unknown to you. If you begin your attacking moves
by trying two or three fast Inner Ankle Throws, it will
prove difficult for him to avoid your attempts and at

FIG. 20

the same time use a throwing action against you. Even if you do not succeed in your efforts to throw him to the mat, you will have at least gained some idea as to the measure of his skill, by the quickness and ease with which he avoids your attacking movements. If you do manage to throw him, that is good enough. On the other hand, if he should stop your attack with ease, you would have to be rather wary of him.

Shoulder Throw (2nd method) (Seoinage)

This type of throwing action may be used together with the Inner Ankle Throw (2nd method). Let us assume that your partner has frustrated your efforts to throw him with the Inner Ankle Throw (2nd method), by taking a lengthy pace backwards with his right foot, and your right hand is situated close to his right thigh. It is not practical to grip his left lapel and use the Shoulder Throw (1st method), due to the time it would take in doing so. Because your partner's right leg is now extended behind him, his upper body is inclined forward, which is a considerable help to you. When your partner steps backwards with his right foot, place the ball of your right foot on the mat in front of his right foot and pull his right arm forward with your left hand. Now pivot on the ball of your right foot round to your left until you face the same direction as your partner, when your left foot can be

FIG. 21

planted on the mat just inside his left foot. As soon as
you complete this turn bend your legs and continue to
pull his right arm forward. At this stage your right hip
should be positioned directly in line with, but below, his
right hip to prevent him stepping forward and outward
with his right leg to avoid being thrown. Bring the crook
of your right arm powerfully upwards against his upper
right arm. On bending your right arm, clench your right
hand so that the action it follows is similar to that of an
'uppercut' in boxing. Continue pulling at your partner's
right jacket sleeve with your left hand and straighten
your legs until your buttocks are thrust upwards against
his stomach (Fig. 21). When he begins to fall over your
right hip, retain the grip on his right sleeve with your left
hand and glide him safely down to the mat in such a
way that he can break the fall with his left arm, just before
his back touches the surface. Keep a good sense of balance by bending your legs and keeping your upper body
upright as your partner falls, in order that you do not fall
with him or, worse still, fall on him. Practise this throwing movement many times, then change roles with your
partner so that he may also practise it.

Group Two

Sweeping Ankle Throw (**Okuriashiharai**) , Body Drop
Throw (**Taitoshi**) and Sweeping Hip Throw (**Haraigoshi**)

Sweeping Ankle Throw (**Okuriashiharai**)
In an effort to make the description of this throwing
movement easier to follow, I have split the Sweeping
Ankle Throw into two parts.

The first part is mainly concerned with the breaking of
your partner's balance while the second part deals chiefly
with the throwing action. Once these separate parts are
mastered individually you should join them together to
accomplish the complete throwing action. Stand facing
one another, holding each other's jackets in the basic
sleeve and lapel grip. Now move slowly sideways to your
left, asking your partner to move in the same direction
as you, by stepping outwards to his right, but making the

elementary mistakes of bringing his left foot too close
to his right and going up on to his toes. After you have
both taken two paces to your left, you must prepare yourself to tilt his upper body over his left leg on the third
pace, a split second before his left foot is brought up to
his right foot. This action is achieved by pulling at his
jacket towards his left ear with your hands and at the
same time bending and straightening your left leg. Remember to tense the muscles of your stomach to add
power to your movements. On the completion of these
combined actions your partner should be lifted right up
on to his toes (Fig. 22). This movement is described
in Judo parlance as a 'floating action'. You will find it

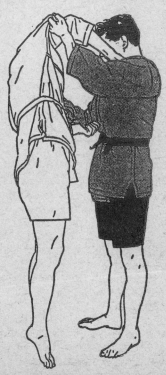

FIG. 22

difficult at first to master the correct timing of your movements, but if you work in harmony with one another,
the moment will come when you suddenly feel that the
timing of your movement is perfected. Now it is best to
let your partner change places with you and practise this
first part of the Sweeping Ankle Throw, before you continue to learn the second part. To avoid wasting time,
there is no need for you to walk back across the mat when
it is your partner's turn to practise breaking your balance.
All that you both have to do is to move in the opposite
direction after you have brought him up on to his toes,
so that he can tilt your upper body over your left leg on
the third step. After you have both gained a reasonable
knowledge of the correct way to break an opponent's balance, you will be ready to carry on and learn the second
half of the Sweeping Ankle Throw.

On breaking your partner's balance on the third step

FIG. 23

bring the sole of your right foot against the outside of his left ankle. Sweep his left leg to your left, keeping the little toe of your right foot nearest the mat and your right leg almost straight. When making this sweeping action with your right foot, keep it as close to the mat as possible by lowering your right hip and inclining your upper body over to the right. As soon as this compound action causes your partner to fall to the mat, glide him on to his back so that he can safely break the fall with his right arm, while retaining the grip on your right sleeve with his left hand. You should keep the grip which you have on his left jacket lapel with your right hand in order to diminish the speed of his fall (Fig. 23).

Body Drop Throw (Taitoshi)
The throwing action known as the Body Drop Throw can be combined very effectively with the Sweeping Ankle Throw which I have just described. Whether an opponent successfully avoids your attempted Sweeping Ankle Throw by bending his left leg or withdrawing his left ankle out of harm's way, in both cases it is necessary for him to support his body weight momentarily on his right leg, which in turn weakens his posture.

Try a Sweeping Ankle Throw against your partner and call on him to avoid it by bending his left leg or moving his left foot backwards. When your partner evades your right foot continue the sweeping action of your right foot. Pivot on the ball of your left foot in a leftward circular direction until you face the same direction as your partner. On the completion of this turn well bend your left leg and place your left foot, with the toes pointing outwards, in front of and outside your partner's left foot. While making these movements with your legs change the pulling motion of your hands, in such a way that instead of tilting his upper body over his left leg you tilt it forward. This is achieved by pulling his right arm across your chest with your left hand and pushing upwards and forwards with your right hand which is gripping his left jacket lapel. Straighten your right leg, and by placing the sole of your right foot on the mat just outside his right foot lodge the back of your right calf in front of his right ankle joint. Keep the outside edge of your right foot

FIG. 24

clear of the mat to ensure that your right knee is turned
slightly downwards and that most of your body weight is
supported by your left leg (Fig. 24). Pull at your partner's right sleeve with your left hand and push at his
left lapel with your right hand until he falls over your
outstretched right leg. Glide him down to the mat on to
his back while retaining your grip on his right sleeve with
your left hand (Fig. 25). Your partner must maintain his
grip on your jacket with his right hand and break the fall
with his left arm just before his back touches the mat.

It is most important during this throwing action for you
to keep your left leg well bent, in order that your hips
are well below the hips of your partner. You should on
no account bend forward too much from the waist. Another essential point for you to notice is that the only
contact you have with your partner is made with your
hands and lower right leg. For example, if you allow him
to push against your right buttock with his right thigh he
may succeed in regaining his balance and consequently

FIG. 25

hinder your throwing action. A very quick-witted opponent may also try to stop this throwing action by bending
his right leg in an effort to stablize his balance, when you
try to lodge your right calf against his right ankle. However, if you make sure that your right knee is always
turned slightly downwards you are still able to complete
the throwing action. There is always the possibility that
an opponent will combat this measure by pressing his
right knee against the back of yours. If such an instance
arises, bend your right leg, giving way to his pressure, and
then straighten both of your legs. On performing this
spring-like action of the legs, you will be able to throw an
opponent with considerable speed. Should a skilful opponent manage to bring his left leg forward before you have
completed the throwing action, it does not affect the result provided you continue to tilt his upper body forward.

Sweeping Hip Throw (**Haraigoshi**)
This throwing technique can be used in combination
with the Sweeping Ankle Throw, as an alternative to the
Body Drop Throw. Let us assume that you have tried to

FIG. 26

bring the sole of your right foot against your partner's
left ankle in an effort to accomplish the Sweeping Ankle
Throw. Your partner on the other hand has successfully
evaded your throwing action by moving his left foot
back. You should ignore this action of his, and continue
your movements by pivoting on the ball of your left foot,
making a counter-clockwise turn to your left. When you
make this turn pull your partner's right arm across your
chest by drawing your left elbow towards your left hip.
With your right hand tug his left lapel towards your right
ear and drive your right elbow underneath his left arm-

pit. When your turning action causes you to face the same direction as your partner, bend your left leg and position your left foot on the mat with the toes pointing slightly outwards, inside but in front of his left foot. Keep your right leg almost straight with the foot pointing downwards and then swing it quickly backwards, contacting the front of his right thigh with the back of your right thigh (Fig. 26). On reaping his right leg from under him in this way, twist your hips sharply to the left, while still continuing to tilt his upper body over the toes of his right foot.

You must glide your partner down to the ground on to his back and retain your grip on his right jacket sleeve, in order to slow down the speed of his fall. He should keep his hold on your left lapel and hit the mat with his left arm just before his back touches the surface.

Group Three

Rear Throw (Osoto-Gari) and Rear Dash Throw (Ni-dan Kosotogari)

Rear Throw (Osoto-Gari)
Stand facing your partner, then take the sleeve and lapel grip on each other's jacket. Ask your partner to keep his feet wide apart, and position yourself in such a way that the toes of his right foot point forward between your feet. Now push your right hand against the left side of his chest and request him to impede this action by inclining his upper body forward. Instead of using greater force to overcome his resistance, use your right hand to pull the left lapel towards the right side of your neck. Incline your upper body towards your front and step smoothly forward on to your slightly bent left leg. Place your left foot about six inches away from the outside edge of his right foot and draw your left elbow outwards past your left side, in such a way that his right arm is drawn across the front of your body, with the bicep muscles of his upper arm pressed against the right side of your chest. Bring your right leg forward between your left leg and his right leg, keeping your foot clear of the mat. Sway your hips slightly to the left in order that you are able to avoid

his right hip, and then lodge your right buttock behind
his right buttock. Now with the foot pointing downwards,
swing your fairly straight right leg backwards and partially outwards as you twist your hips slightly to the left, to
ensure that contact is made against his body with the back
of your right thigh and right buttock (Fig. 27). When he
begins to fall change the slightly upward pulling motion
of your right hand into a strong downward pushing one
(Fig. 28). Take care to glide your partner to the mat so
that he lands squarely on his back and is able to break
the fall by using his left arm. For the purpose of slowing
down the speed of his fall you should keep the grip that
you have on his right jacket sleeve with your left hand.

FIG. 27

I consider it worth while to give a short summary, se-
lecting the most important details that go to make up this
particular throwing movement.

This is an instance of a technique that relies upon the
reactions of an opponent. First you gently push against
his chest with your right hand, until he resists by pushing
back at you. You then pull his upper body towards you
and step forward on to your bent left leg. On the occasion
that you step forward he will in all probability lean backwards to counteract the pulling movement of your hands.
Consequently when you suddenly change the pulling
movement of your right hand into a downward push and
make the sweeping action with your right leg, he will be
unwittingly assisting your throwing action by leaning backwards.

Rear Dash Throw (Ni-dan Kosotogari)

This technique is appropriate for use against an opponent who has succeeded in evading your attempted Rear
Throw, by lifting his right leg over your oncoming right

FIG. 28

leg. I must point out, however, that if this happens it proves that the opponent's balance was not properly disturbed at the onset. This throwing action can also be used by itself when an opponent persistently turns his right side nearest to you, when about to try attacking movements against your right side.

Try to perform a Rear Throw against your partner and request him to avoid your right leg by raising his right foot from the ground. After he eludes your right leg, quickly place your right foot down on the mat. Twisting your upper body slightly to the right, advance your left hip and bring your left foot forward in a clockwise circular movement. Now pull your partner's right sleeve towards your left hip and at the same time push your right hand (which is gripping his left lapel) forward and downwards against his left collar-bone. Continuing to advance your left hip, bring the sole of your left foot powerfully against the back of his left ankle and use your hands to bend him over backwards (Fig. 29). As soon as your

FIG. 29

partner falls, take great care to glide him down on to his
back, still keeping the grip that you have on his right
jacket sleeve with your left hand, so that he may safely
break the fall with his left arm.

There are two mistakes that are very often made by
beginners in Judo while practising this throwing movement. The first mistake is that they allow their right leg
to continue the reaping movement for too long after an
opponent has managed to evade it. If you should fall
into this error your right foot would be situated too far
in front of your opponent's right foot for the successful
application of the Rear Dash Throw. This in turn leads
to another error, which is that of attempting to sweep
an opponent's left leg from under him, after he has been
able to increase his sense of balance by replacing his right
foot on to the mat.

Group Four

Drawing Ankle Throw (Tsurikomiashi) and Knee Wheel Throw (Hizaguruma)

Drawing Ankle Throw (Tsurikomiashi)
Stand facing each other and grasp one another's jacket
with the sleeve and lapel grip. Push your left hand against
your partner's right arm and invite him to resist this action, by pushing back against the left side of your chest
with his right hand and advancing his right leg. As soon
as you begin to feel his resistance increasing, step a small
pace to your right with your right leg, placing your right
foot on the mat with the toes pointing slightly inwards.
Now tug your partner's upper body forward and upwards
by drawing your hands towards your left ear. By these
movements you will cause the weight of his body to be
poised over the toes of his right foot, which will generally
make him react by attempting to step forward with his
right foot in an effort to adjust his balance. At the same
time as he prepares to make this step you should speedily
bring the sole of your left foot against the front of his
right ankle (Fig. 30). Withdraw your left hip and con-

tinue to tilt his upper body forward over the toes of his
right foot. When he trips over your foot you must glide
him down towards the mat, maintaining the pull at his
right jacket sleeve with your left hand, and as he is falling
twist him over on to his back, so that he may safely
break the fall with his left arm. At the same time he
should continue to hold on to your left jacket lapel with
his right hand, whilst you keep the grip on his right jacket
sleeve with your left hand.

I have found that the most common mistake which a
beginner makes is to leave the left side of his body forward for longer than is necessary. If you fall into this
error it would give an opponent the chance to regain
his balance, by pushing against the left side of your
chest with his right hand.

Knee Wheel Throw (Hizaguruma)

The Knee Wheel Throw can be used when an opponent

FIG. 30

consistently avoids an attempted Drawing Ankle Throw
by raising his leg above your oncoming foot. I have good
reason to know that this form of evasion is unwise to use
too many times. When my grade was Orange Belt (4th
Kyu), I was asked to practise by a friend who had noticed
that I was in the habit of raising my right leg whenever
a person tried to throw me with a Drawing Ankle Throw.
Shortly after starting the practice my friend brought his
left foot towards my right ankle, while I as usual lifted
my foot to step over his oncoming foot. Suddenly I found
that the sole of his left foot was pressing against the outside of my right knee and I was thrown to the mat with a
Knee Wheel Throw. This encounter was a lesson to me
and it taught me how foolhardy it is to always use the
same method of defence or attack, without some vari-
ations.

Give your partner the impression that you intend to
use a Drawing Ankle Throw against him, by bringing
your left foot towards the front of his right ankle. Ask him
to avoid your advancing foot by raising his right foot
from the mat. When his right leg is poised in the air,
quickly raise your left leg still more until you are able to
press the sole of your left foot against the outside of his
right knee (Fig. 31). Continue pulling at his jacket with
your hands, while twisting your upper body to the left
and push the sole of your left foot firmly against the
outside of his right knee. When your movements cause
him to fall over your left foot, make sure that you glide
him down on to his back so that he may safely break the
fall with his left arm. You should maintain a grip on his
jacket sleeve with your left hand while he continues to
hold your left jacket lapel with his right hand. If you are
trying this throwing movement against an opponent without combining it with the Drawing Ankle Throw, your
aim should be to attack his right knee just before his
weight is placed on to his right leg. This means that as
you are moving about the mat together you must wait
for the opportunity when he is advancing his right leg
towards you, in order that you can press the sole of your
left foot against the outside of his right knee and tilt his
upper body over his right leg, just before he firmly plants
his right foot on to the mat.

FIG. 31

Group Five

Left-Sleeve Hip Throw (Hidari-Tsurikomigoshi) and Inner Thigh Throw (Uchimata)

Left-Sleeve Hip Throw **(Hidari-Tsurikomigoshi)**
Stand facing your partner and hold each other's jacket in
the basic sleeve and lapel grip. Start your movements
by pushing your partner's right sleeve downwards with
your left hand and request him to resist this pressure by
raising his right arm. After he begins to raise his arm stop
the downward push and start to lift his right arm upwards
with your left hand. Pull at his left jacket lapel with your
right hand as you raise his right arm above the level of
his shoulders. Keep your left arm slightly bent and tuck

FIG. 32

your left elbow underneath his right armpit. Step forward
with your left leg and place the ball of your left foot
on the mat just inside his left foot (Fig. 32). Pivoting on
the ball of your left foot, turn your body in a clockwise
direction until you are facing the same way as your partner, when you will be able to plant your right foot firmly
on the mat just inside his right foot (Fig. 33). Now well
bend your legs and make certain that your back is turned
squarely to him, in such a way that you check any effort
he might make to step forward or outward with his left
leg, by pressing the left side of your lower back against
the left side of his stomach. Straighten your legs and continue pushing his right arm upwards past the left side of
your face while still pulling firmly at his left jacket lapel
with your right hand. These movements will cause your

FIG. 33

FIG. 34

partner to be lifted into the air and you should make
him fall to the ground over your left hip by twisting your
upper body sharply to the right. Once he is falling release the hold that you have on his right sleeve and make
certain that you glide him down to the mat, squarely
on to his back so that he can safely break the fall with his
right arm. Meanwhile he should retain the grip he has on
your right jacket sleeve with his left hand to help decrease
the speed of his fall (Fig. 34).

Inner Thigh Throw **(Uchimata)**
Stand opposite your partner and take the sleeve and lapel
grip on each other's jacket. Push your partner's right arm
upwards with your left hand and twist your hips slightly
to the right, giving him the false impression that you in-

FIG. 35

tend to use a Sleeve Hip Throw against him. Call on him
to oppose your movements by forcing his right arm downwards and at the same time bending his legs. Instead of
trying to overcome this opposition on his part, change the
form of your attack and turn his forceful resistance to
your own advantage. Do this by suddenly moving your
right leg forward until you can place the ball of your
right foot on the mat close to the inside of his right foot.
Now divert the strength that he is using to push his right
arm downwards, by pulling his right sleeve forward with
your left hand. Draw him towards you by tightening your
grip on his left jacket lapel and bending your right arm,
until your clenched fist is close to the right side of your
face (Fig. 35). Pivot to your left on the ball of your
right foot by withdrawing your left side, until you can
plant your left foot firmly on to the mat close to the inside of his left foot. When you bring your left leg backwards drive your right elbow underneath his left armpit
and bring the left side of your lower back into contact
with the left side of his stomach. Now raise your right
foot off the mat, then keeping your right leg almost
straight with the foot pointing downwards, thrust it backwards in between his legs and continue to pull at his
jacket, so that his weight is situated over the toes of his
right foot. Hoist him up with your hands to such an extent that his legs are brought astride your right buttock
(Fig. 36). Sweep upwards and outwards with your right
leg, bringing the outside of your right thigh into contact
with the inside of his right thigh. As soon as your partner
begins to fall over your outstretched right leg, glide him
down to the mat on his back by pulling his right arm
across the front of your body and pushing his left
shoulder downwards with your right hand. He must break
the fall by striking the mat with his left arm and you
must maintain the grip on his right sleeve with your left
hand to retard the impetus of his fall.

The method just given would not be suitable for you if
your height is six feet or more. This is because you would
find it awkward to get very close to a shorter adversary
and at the same time get your hips below his. For this
reason, if you are tall you would sometimes be well ad-
vised to place greater emphasis on the action of your

FIG. 36

right leg, rather than relying on the action of your body. Because of the length of your legs you need not place your left foot quite so close to an opponent's left foot, but for this very reason you must be careful that you do not kick him when you sweep upwards with your right leg. Another important adjustment for you to make is that when you use the sweeping action of your right leg the contact is made at the back of your right thigh and the inside of his **left** thigh.

Group Six

Basic Hip Throws (Ogoshi), Stomach Throw **(Tomoenage)** and Corner Throw **(Sumi-Gaeshi)**

Basic Hip Throw (*1st method*) **(Ogoshi)**

Take the fundamental sleeve and lapel grip on your partner's jacket and invite him to hold your jacket in the same way. Push against his right sleeve with your left hand and ask him to oppose this action, by in turn pushing back against the left side of your chest with his right

FIG. 37

hand. As soon as he tries to stop your movements in this way continue by pulling his right arm forward with your left hand, keeping your left arm slightly bent. Still maintaining the pulling motion of your left hand, turn your body round to the left by pivoting on the ball of your right foot, then drive your right elbow underneath his left armpit. When you complete this counter-clockwise turning action of your body and come to face the same direction as your partner, position your left foot on the mat just inside his left foot. Well bend your legs and ensure that your right hip is directly in line with his right hip. You should support most of your body weight on your bent left leg, keeping the toes of your left foot pointing slightly outwards to increase your sense of balance. Continue to draw your partner up on to his toes by pulling his right arm across the front of your body with your left hand and pulling his left lapel towards your right ear

FIG. 38

and with your right hand. Now straighten your legs and thrust your buttocks upwards against his stomach. As soon as this powerful movement causes his feet to leave the ground, twist your hips to the left and continue to pull him over your right hip (Fig. 37). You must maintain the grip that you have on his right jacket sleeve with your left hand, in order to restrict the speed of his fall. Your partner should keep his hold of your left jacket lapel with his right hand and break the fall by slapping the mat with his left arm (Fig. 38).

Basic Hip Throw (*2nd Method*) (**Ogoshi**)

This variation of the Hip Throw has been devised for the use of a person who is confronted by a shorter opponent. (Some high grades of Judo do not consider this 2nd Method of the Hip Throw to be quite so skilful as the 1st Method just given.)

Ask your partner to take hold of your right jacket sleeve with his left hand and grasp your left jacket lapel with his right hand. You should grip his right jacket sleeve with your left hand, then slide the thumb of your right hand inside the back of his jacket collar and obtain a firm hold on his jacket at the nape of his neck. Push against your partner's right sleeve with your left hand and call on him to oppose this action of yours by push-

FIG. 39

ing against the left side of your chest with his right hand and leaning his upper body towards you. To disturb your partner's balance pull his right arm forward with your left hand and to make his posture even more insecure bend your right arm and force his head forward, by pressing the crook of your right arm against the back of his neck. Bring your right leg forward and place the ball of your right foot on the mat just inside his right foot. Pivoting round to your left on the ball of your right foot, carry on pulling his right arm across the front of your chest and make sure that you do not allow him to free his head from within the crook of your right arm. On turning enough to face the same direction as your partner place your left foot on the mat just inside his left foot, then well bend your legs and make certain that most of your body weight is supported on your bent left leg. Straighten your legs and twist your hips to the left so that your partner is thrown over your right hip (Fig. 39). When your partner falls to the mat take care to guide him on to his back in order that he may break the fall with his left arm. You should unwind your right arm from around his neck and use your grip on his right sleeve to slow down the speed of his fall.

Stomach Throw (Tomoenage)

This is an ideal throwing technique when it is used against an opponent who tries to fluster you by rushing at you. Alternatively it can be brought into play against a person who adopts a semi-defensive crouch in an effort to force a draw. Unfortunately, this throwing action is all too often used by exponents who favour the section of Judo known as Groundwork, which covers ways of contesting from the lying or kneeling position, and they simply use the Stomach Throw as a poor excuse for dragging an opponent down to the ground. I have noticed that when a participant of a contest uses this throwing action it is generally as a last desperate effort on his part to score against his opponent. Nevertheless when a Stomach Throw is correctly used and carried out at the right moment it is successful. One occasion when this throwing method can be used to good effect is when it is used in conjunction with a Hip Throw.

Before you attempt the throwing movement against your partner, it is most important to make sure that he has completely mastered the 5th Method in the section covering How to Break a Fall on page 28.

Adopt the basic sleeve and lapel grips on one another's

jacket. Give a sharp push at your partner's right jacket
sleeve with your left hand and pull his left jacket lapel
towards you with your right hand. These movements will
cause his left side to be turned nearest to you. Step a
small pace forward with your left foot as though you
intend to use a Hip Throw against him. Ask him to resist
the contrary actions of your hands by pushing forward
against the left side of your chest with his right hand and
pulling at your right jacket sleeve with his left hand.
These actions of his will mean that he takes back his left
side and advances his right side, in an effort to squarely
face you. When he turns to face you, then is the crucial
moment for you to weaken his posture. Do this by keeping
your clenched hands turned inwards at the wrist and
drawing him up on to his toes with an inclined lifting
action. Begin to bend your left leg and bring the sole
of your right foot upwards against his stomach, with the
toes turned slightly outwards (Fig. 40). Bend your left
leg even more and sit down on the mat close to your left

FIG. 40

heel while continuing to pull your partner forward, ensuring that you keep your forearms almost in line with your shoulders. As soon as your partner loses his balance completely and pitches forward over you, partially straighten your bent right leg and pull downwards with your hands so that you can throw him head over heels to the mat beyond your head.

On progressing to the stage where you throw your partner, make certain that you release your right hand from his left jacket lapel at the last moment, so that he is able to roll safely on to his back (Fig. 41). Your partner should step past your left side with his right leg to such an extent that he can roll forward over your body as you recline to the ground, and beat the mat with his left arm just before his back touches the surface.

Corner Throw (Sumi-Gaeshi)

If your attempt to throw an opponent with a Stomach Throw has failed, you can follow it up by using a Corner Throw. Under the present rules of Judo a participant of a contest is not allowed to drag his opponent to the

FIG. 41

ground for the sole purpose of beginning Groundwork. When he has not succeeded in breaking the opponent's balance by using a Stomach Throw or similar technique, he must regain his upright posture and continue the contest from a standing position. This does not mean to say that his opponent need allow him to stand up, as he could follow him to the mat and use a Groundwork technique against him.

Let us presume that you are lying on the mat after your partner has successfully avoided your attempted Stomach Throw by stepping outwards to his right, thus causing the sole of your right foot to glance off his left hip. Without hesitation press home your attack with the following throwing movement.

Slide your left heel along the mat until you are able to lodge the inside part of your left lower leg against the outside of his right ankle. Turn partially on to your left side and position your right foot in between his legs, pressing your right instep against the inside of his left thigh. Pull your partner downwards with both hands towards the direction of your left ear and push your right instep outwards and slightly forward against the inside of

FIG. 42

his upper left thigh. Use the lower part of your left leg to block his right leg and prevent him from moving it in his efforts to escape the throwing movement. As soon as your partner trips over your lower left leg and begins to fall, you must take great care to glide him down to the mat safely on to his back (Fig. 42). Do this by pulling up at his right jacket sleeve at the last moment and pushing your right hand firmly against the left side of his chest. Your partner should break the fall with his left arm just before his back touches the mat.

It should be noted that this type of throwing action is very usefully employed against an opponent who is standing by your feet after you have stumbled, or been tripped to the ground, without the conditions of a point being fulfilled.

7 / GETTING UP AFTER BEING THROWN TO THE GROUND

ON EACH occasion that an opponent throws you to the ground, it is most important for you to guard against his using a surprise attacking movement when you regain your feet. Although you must be allowed to get on to your feet after having been properly thrown, it would not be considered ungentlemanly conduct on the part of your opponent if he was to give you a seemingly helping hand and to throw you back to the mat in a vigorous manner immediately you stand upright. It must be noted, however, that this trick would be frowned on if you were merely practising together. Provided you study the correct way of rising from the ground there is little chance of falling victim to this dodge in a contest.

Call on your partner to throw you to the mat with one of the throwing movements already explained. After breaking your fall bring your feet nearest to him so that you could use them to ward him off if necessary. Turn partially on to your right side and place the palm of your right hand on the mat close to your right hip. Now draw your bent right leg underneath your body and raise yourself from the mat on to your feet by straightening your right arm. Once you have raised yourself into a crouching posture, position your left forearm in front of your chest, keeping it parallel to the ground, with the fingers of your left hand pointing towards your right. Continue to move backwards from your partner while straightening your legs, in order that you regain an upright posture some little distance way from him.

After you have mastered this technique and are able to perform it at speed, change roles with your partner to accord him a chance of practising the movement.

8 / OVERCOMING A DEFENSIVE OPPONENT

SHOULD you be confronted by a very defensive opponent who is of similar standard in skill, it will often be very difficult for you to overcome his resistance and so throw him. It should be appreciated at the same time, however, that he cannot throw you whilst he is intent on using defensive tactics. A person who uses this negative style of Judo usually holds his opponent's jacket lapels with both hands and keeps his legs well bent. There are several throwing techniques which may be used by you in an effort to overcome this defensive posture, some of which have already been explained. These are Corner Throw, Knee Wheel Throw, Inner Ankle Throw, Inner Thigh Throw, and Stomach Throw. The Inner Ankle Throw is one of the best attacking moves to use when trying to pierce an opponent's defence, because it is not easy to counter with a throwing technique. Provided you grip his lapels, making sure that your arms are inside his, it is possible to lever his arms outwards with your elbows and so considerably aid you in your efforts to throw him. As soon as you force his arms outwards you should attack with three or four fast Inner Ankle Throws in order to fluster him and create an opening for one of the major throwing actions, such as the Inner Thigh Throw. After practising the throwing actions already outlined for use against a defensive opponent, study the following three additional throwing movements and three standing armlocks. Although your partner should get into a defensive crouch, he must not offer too much resistance in the early phases of training. Moreover, after you have both temporarily adopted the role of a defender, do not make the mistake of using it each time that you practise, otherwise you will retard your own progress in the art.

Valley Drop Throw **(Taniotoshi)**
Stand facing one another, then request your partner to
get into a defensive crouch and take his grips on your
jacket. You should keep an upright stance and obtain
the basic sleeve and lapel grip on his jacket. Under no
circumstances should you sacrifice your speed of movement by crouching, or grasping his jacket too tightly.

Position yourself in such a way that the toes of your
partner's right foot point forward between your feet. Now
by leaning slightly backwards pull him towards you and
ask him to resist this action by pressing his toes against
the mat and leaning backwards (Fig. 43). Maintaining
your pulling actions, slide your left heel along the mat in
a forward clockwise movement and fully bend your right

FIG. 43

leg as you recline to the mat on to your left buttock. Just as you lower your body to the mat pull your partner's right sleeve downwards with your left hand and push against the left side of his chest with your right hand. Your left calf should be lodged against the outside of his right heel so that he is forced to fall over it and break the fall with his left arm (Fig. 44). You must ensure that he drops safely on to his back, by retaining your grip on his right jacket sleeve.

There is no necessity to keep throwing your partner; the only essential things to master are the movements leading up to the final throwing action.

Hock Throw (Seoinage)

Ask your partner to adopt a defensive posture by well bending his legs and grasping your jacket lapels. You should hold his jacket in the fundamental sleeve and lapel grip while maintaining an upright stance. Position yourself so that the toes of his right foot point between your feet. Begin to pull him towards you and ask him to resist by in turn pulling back. As soon as he resists in this way step a small pace forward on to your bent left leg and bring the back of your right ankle just below the

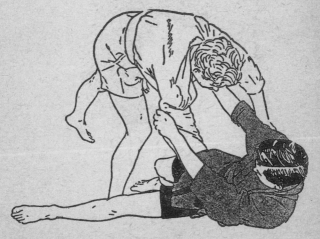

FIG. 44

back of his right knee. Curve your upper body forward, changing the pulling motion of your right hand into a downward push towards his right heel and pull his right arm to your left by drawing your left elbow towards your left hip. Well bend your right leg in order that you can hook his right lower leg forward from under him with your right heel (Fig. 45). After the contrary action of your hands and right leg cause him to fall, take care to see that you glide him down on to his back. He should break the fall with his left arm, while retaining a grip on your jacket with his right hand to restrict his speed of fall.

Side Dash Throw **(Yoko-Gake)**
Invite your partner to get into a defensive posture, with

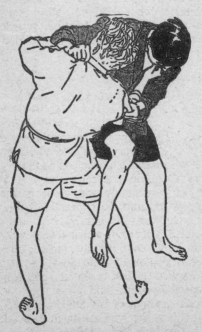

FIG. 45

hands gripping your jacket lapels, whilst you keep an up-right stance and obtain the primary sleeve and lapel grip on his jacket, ensuring that the toes of his left foot point forward between your feet. Now bring the sole of your right foot against the outer bone of his left ankle and pull at his jacket, in order to tilt his upper body over his left leg. At the time that you put these movements into effect bend your left leg and sink to the mat to add the weight of your falling body to the sweeping movement of your right foot. Take care to glide your partner down to the mat on to his back in order that he can safely break the fall with his right arm.

Reverse the instructions where required and perform the throwing movement against his right side.

You will have noticed that this throwing action is similar to the Sweeping Ankle Throw already described, the main difference being that you fall with your partner in this technique, while keeping your body fairly rigid. Should you wish to break the fall with your left arm you are still counted as the thrower and awarded a point in a contest.

Standing Armlocks
The section of Judo concerned with methods of creating a lock on an opponent's elbow joint whilst he is in the standing position are technically termed as Standing Arm-locks. They are most suitable for use against an adversary who grips your jacket very tightly, or alternatively against an opponent who walks towards you at the beginning of a contest or practice, in a careless way. If you practise these armlocks consistently with your partner you will not be liable to fall into the regrettable habit of clasping each other's clothing too tightly, with the consequent slowing down of movement which results when groups of muscles are kept continuously tensed. It should be noted that this section of Judo does not bring good results when applied against a skilful Judo exponent, who keeps an upright posture and grips your jacket loosely until the exact moment of his attack. Should you visit a Judo club it is best that you ask them to define the ruling about these standing locks before bringing them into play. Many clubs do not favour them at all, which is an

error, in my opinion, as it tends to let beginners use a bad style of Judo, without realizing their elementary mistake.

The three basic locks which are explained should be mastered in order that you can apply them with speed when a favourable opportunity arises. Your partner must submit immediately that he feels the slightest discomfort by calling out 'stop' or by tapping your body with the palm of his free hand.

1st Method

Stand facing your partner and ask him to grasp your jacket in the basic sleeve and lapel grip, while you hold his clothing in a similar way. Ask your partner to grip your jacket very tightly and keep his arms bent. Quickly relinquish your hold on his left jacket lapel and step a small pace forward with your right foot. Bring your right hand over and then underneath his upper left arm in a clockwise circular movement. When you make this movement use the crook of your right elbow to force his left elbow joint inwards and upwards, making his left arm become almost fully bent. Now place the palm of your right hand over the inside of your left wrist and obtain a tight grip. Apply enough pressure to make him submit by bringing your right elbow towards your left side, while slightly raising your left arm and left shoulder (Fig. 46). Immediately your partner feels the slightest discomfort

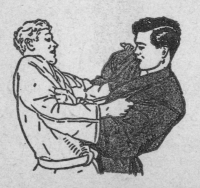

FIG. 46

he must submit by calling out, or lightly tapping your body with his right hand.

2nd Method

This way of causing a person's arm to become locked is most suitable for use as a combination technique against an opponent who prevents you from bending his left arm by forcefully straightening it at the last moment.

You should stand facing one another and hold each other's jacket in the basic sleeve and lapel grip. Free your right hand from your partner's left jacket lapel and begin to swing your right forearm in a clockwise circular direction around his upper left arm. Ask your partner to resist this movement by forcefully straightening his left arm. To counter this opposition you must immediately let go

FIG. 47

of his jacket with your left hand and lodge the outside of your right wrist underneath the back of his left elbow. Keeping your right elbow close against your right side to trap his lower left arm, cup the palm of your left hand around the top of his left shoulder and grip your left wrist with your right hand. To cause his elbow joint to become locked press forward against his left shoulder with the palm of your left hand and bring your lower right arm upwards against the back of his left elbow joint (Fig. 47). To add power to your movements you should lean slightly backwards, but take care to see that your left hand continues to press forward against his left shoulder, in order that a contrary action is used against his left arm.

Your partner must submit when you apply the lock and you must be careful to use steady pressure against his elbow joint.

3rd Method
When faced by a heavier opponent of similar skill who insists on sliding his thumb inside the back of your collar to obtain a firm grip with his right hand at the nape of your neck, it often proves difficult to throw him, especially if he uses a defensive crouch as well. This is due to the fact that his hold about your neck will tend to slow down the speed of your movements and accordingly give him a slight advantage over you. You will remember that this type of hold was touched upon in the section of Combination Throws, where it was pointed out that it is not considered a particularly skilful form of grip.

Ask your partner to obtain his grips on your jacket at the back of your collar with his right hand and underneath your right elbow with his left hand. You should use the basic sleeve and lapel grip on his jacket. Begin your movements by releasing the hold of your left hand from his right jacket sleeve and withdrawing your right hip. On your continuing to make a clockwise turn to your right by pivoting on the ball of your left foot, bring your slightly bent left arm upwards and outside his right arm. Now imagine that you are attempting to deliver a slow punch to the right side of his chin with your left fist, by bringing the crook of your left arm against his upper right arm. You should stop his wrist from moving in the same direction by blocking it with the left side of your neck. Meanwhile you should continue turning to your right until you face the same direction as he is facing. To cause his elbow joint to become locked clasp your hands together then bring the inside part of your left elbow joint inwards against the outside of his right elbow and incline your upper body a trifle to your left (Fig. 48).

You should not try to perform this technique at speed until you are quite sure of the movement and have become used to judging the exact amount of pressure needed to cause your partner to submit. Remember to help one another as much as possible, so that you both progress rapidly.

FIG. 48

9 / DEFENCE AGAINST THROWING ACTIONS

THERE are two main forms of defence against throwing actions. One is based on the principle of offering strong resistance (Fusegi), while the other system is founded on the basis of avoiding and counter-throwing (Kaeshi-Waza). I think it would be foolhardy to be dogmatic and claim that one system is superior to the other. Ideally the principle of avoiding a powerful throwing action and counter-throwing an opponent is following closely on the idea of non-resistance to force which is the nucleus from which Judo has evolved. Due to the fact that an opponent of equal skill may be of lighter weight, heavier, or of similar build, it is sometimes necessary to vary your strategy accordingly. For example, if your opponent is smaller than you, it usually follows that he is capable of moving faster than you are, especially if you are well matched in standard and skill. Consequently, if you use the system of avoiding and counter-throwing, it may be extremely difficult for you to move fast enough to elude his throwing actions. It would therefore be a good policy to use blocking tactics against him by utilizing your greater weight. Conversely, if you are practising with an opponent who is physically superior to yourself, but of equal skill, it would prove unwise to attempt offering resistance, as his greater weight and strength would overcome this form of defence. In this event it would probably prove more advantageous to you if you were to use evasive measures. The principle of non-resistance to force in Judo is often likened to the willow tree in a gale which bends with the force of each gust of wind. Nevertheless if there is a very mild breeze blowing the 'willow tree' need not bend at all!

This is the strategy. If an opponent of similar skill is slightly built, block his throwing actions, but if he happens

to be thickset, avoid them. In the unlikely event of his being of exactly the same size, strength and skill you could
use either method with the same chances of success. I
have selected certain moves from the two basic defensive systems and these should give you a general picture
of the ways of countering a throwing action. You will
realize that all these methods of defence are only prac-
ticable when an opponent does not succeed in breaking
your balance properly at the onset of his attacking movements.

STANDING DEFENCE AGAINST A SMALL OPPONENT
Defence (Fusegi)

Forward Defence (1st Method)

Stand facing your partner, then hold his jacket with the
sleeve and lapel grip and request him to obtain the same
holds on your jacket. Ask him to try the Basic Hip Throw
against your right side in slow motion. Do not attempt to
balk his throwing action by leaning backwards and pushing at his jacket with your hands. It is imperative to keep
an upright posture, otherwise you would invite being
thrown in another direction. Just before his lower back is
brought into contact with your stomach twist your hips
slightly to your left and bring you right knee inwards towards your left knee. Due to these movements your partner's right buttock will touch the outside part of your
right thigh and your right hip. After you have practised
advancing your right hip slowly for a few minutes to
counter your partner's gentle throwing actions, ask him
to increase the speed and power of his movements to
such a degree that you have to bring your right hip and
thigh powerfully forward against the outside of his right
thigh to prevent him from throwing you (Fig. 49). You
should keep your head held back and hold your breath
just before you block his movements.

After you have mastered this technique, change roles
with your partner so that he may also practise blocking
your attempted throwing actions.

Should a smaller opponent attempt to throw you to
the mat with an Inner Thigh Throw, it would not be feasi-

ble to use your hip to neutralize his attack. What you would have to do in this case would be to walk forward while keeping your head pressed back.

Call on your partner to start an Inner Thigh Throw against you in slow motion. When he sweeps upwards with his right or left leg in between your legs, keep your weight situated over your heels and push him downwards

FIG. 49

and forward with your hands. Keep perfectly upright with your head held back and then walk forward into your partner, while using your hands to push him face forward to the mat. Provided you always remember to hold your head back it will make it somewhat difficult for an opponent to break your balance when trying to throw you in a forward direction, but you must be careful to see that he does not suddenly change the direction of his attack and so throw you backwards to the mat.

Freeing an Arm (2nd Method)

This type of defence can be used to advantage against a physically weaker opponent, who uses the basic sleeve and lapel grip on your jacket for implementing forward throwing actions against you.

Obtain the sleeve and lapel grip on one another's jackets, then ask your partner to try a Shoulder Throw against your right side in slow time. When he steps forward with his right foot and prepares to make a counter-clockwise turn to his left you must put your defensive

FIG. 50

movements into effect. Withdraw your right hip by stepping a pace backwards with your right leg, so that you are sideways to him, with your left side nearest him. As soon as you put this movement into effect you may thrust your left clenched hand against his right jacket sleeve and free your right sleeve from the grasp of his left hand by forcefully bending your right arm. The role of your left hand is to stop your partner from gaining the essential body contact, while your right arm is freed from the grip of his left hand to prevent him from winding you around his body (Fig. 50). You will find the timing of these movements difficult to master at first, but with practice you will gradually be able to use the correct timing essential for success.

Interposing a Foot (3rd Method)

Stand facing your partner and take the sleeve and lapel grip on each other's jacket. Invite him to try a Sweeping Hip Throw against your right side by bringing his right thigh backwards against your right leg. When he turns to face the same direction as you are facing and brings

FIG. 51

his right leg backwards against yours, place all of your body weight on to your slightly bent right leg. On momentarily blocking his throwing action in this way, raise your left foot from the mat and pass it forward between his legs. Immediately you succeed in getting your left foot in front of his lower left leg, turn your foot outwards so that the toes point to your left, and press the outside edge of your foot against the front of his left ankle joint. In conjunction with these movements you must keep an upright stance, and prevent your partner's lower back from making contact with your body by pushing at his jacket with your hands (Fig. 51). After you have accomplished these movements it will make him give up his efforts to use this particular throwing action. He should not attempt to force a conclusion, as it would only result in his falling face forward to the mat. On no account must you use your lower left leg to sweep backwards against the front of his left leg, although it is permissible to use your lower leg as an alternative to your left foot for checking his actions.

This is one of the many techniques which can be reversed. Consequently change the instructions where necessary so that you block your partner's efforts to use a throwing action against your left thigh.

Lifting an Opponent (4th Method)

This defence can be brought into play against an opponent of small build who is fond of using Hip Throws.

Take up the normal sleeve and lapel grips on one another's jacket, and ask your partner to try one of the Hip Throws against your right side in slow motion. Begin your counter movements by bending your legs and releasing your holds on his jacket immediately he begins to make his turning action for the throwing technique. Keeping your feet firmly planted on to the mat, hug his upper body with both arms and press him to you. Now partially straighten your legs and thrust your stomach forward against his buttocks (Fig. 52). When your movements cause him to be lifted bodily from the ground, as though he were sitting in your lap, shuffle backwards with your feet and gently drop him to the ground. As soon as he begins to fall you must quickly grasp his

FIG. 52

right sleeve with your left hand, in order to glide him down to the mat safely on to his back. He for his part should break the fall with his left arm.

You may find it difficult at first to lift your partner from the ground. This is because, due to the slowness of your movements, he would have plenty of time to set himself. When you progress to the stage where he moves at speed, your counter should be applied just prior to his final throwing action. This means that as he prepares to pivot on his right (or left) foot you begin to scoop him upwards.

One mistake a beginner makes is to rely solely on the lifting power of his arms to counter an opponent, instead of using the lifting power of his legs, coupled with the powerful forward and upward surging movement of his stomach.

pper left
left hand should
hile the tops of your
is upper thigh. Due to
part of an anchor, your
bring you over his right leg
aid your counter measures it is best to

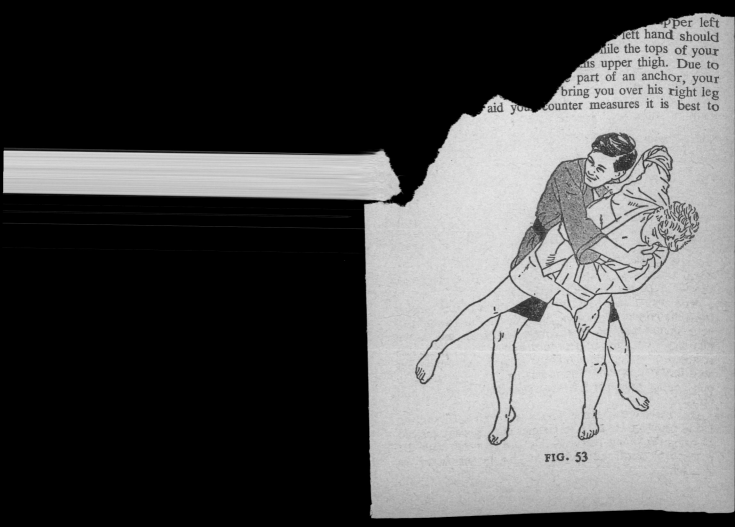

FIG. 53

Moving in the O[...]

This form of defen[...] accomplis[...]
forward throwing actio[...] of *Inner Th[...]*
sition, with the exception [...] *lapel grip* [...]

Take up the sleeve and [...]
jacket and invite your part[...] to try [...]
Throw against your right side. When he puts [...]
body weight on to his bent left leg, just prior [...]
the throwing action into effect, push his upper [...]
rectly to your left and step a pace in the same di[...]

FIG. 54

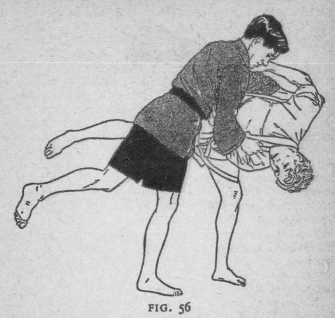

FIG. 56

this makes it impossible for him to get his right leg in between yours (Fig. 56). Once you have succeeded in avoiding his leg in this way it is a simple matter to counter-throw him. All that you have to do is to pull his left lapel towards your right and push his right sleeve forward. These movements will cause him to be twisted over on to his back. You must permit him to break the fall with his right arm by releasing your left hand from his jacket sleeve as he begins to fall.

It is sometimes essential to use your lower left leg to stop a reasonably skilled opponent from hopping forward on his left foot in an effort to stabilize his balance. This stratagem is achieved by sliding your left leg outwards to the left and placing your left foot on the mat close to the outside of your opponent's left foot, immediately after you have successfully avoided the sweeping action of his right leg. Against a very powerful opponent, however, it will usually suffice to throw him if you simply use your hands. The reason for this is that he will be

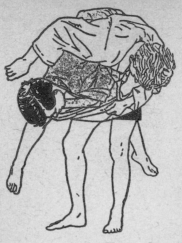

FIG. 57

unable to stop the movement of his right leg quickly
enough after you have avoided it. You should practise
avoiding your partner's leg over and over again, as once
you have become skilled at this form of evasion it only
remains for you to synchronize the movement of your
hands to bring about his downfall as his body roughly
conforms to the letter T. After you have become pro-
ficient at avoiding your partner's right leg reverse the instructions where necessary and practise evading his left
leg.

Countering a Hip Throw
Take up the basic sleeve and lapel grip on one another's
jacket and call on your partner to attempt a Hip Throw
against your right side. When he endeavours to place his
right foot on the mat close by the inside of your right foot
you should release your left hand from his right jacket
sleeve and step outwards to your right with your right
foot. Pass your left arm around his waist and bring your
left leg close to your right leg without allowing your left
foot to contact the mat. Once you have rounded his
lower back and right hip in this way, bring your left leg
in front of him and position your left foot on the mat

FIG. 58

just inside his left foot. Follow this up by bringing your right foot just inside his right foot while holding him close to you with your hands. At this juncture you should well bend your legs and ensure that your right leg supports most of your body weight. To accomplish the counter-throwing action, straighten your legs, twist your hips to the right and pull his upper body forward by tugging at his left lapel with your right hand (Fig. 57). He should break the fall with his right arm and you must take care to glide him to the mat on to his back.

You will find this counter stroke difficult to master, but provided you spare no effort you will gradually become used to it. In a competitive practice it is not always essential to have your back turned squarely to an opponent when accomplishing a 'left side' Hip Throw as a retaliatory throwing action. This is due to the fact that an opponent's body will be in a tensed state during his exertions to throw you, and provided you manage to achieve contact at the right side of his stomach with your left buttock it will cause all of his body to be affected.

Countering a Sweeping Ankle Throw

Secure the sleeve and lapel grip on each other's jacket and call on your partner to try a Sweeping Ankle Throw against your right leg (which should be in advance of your left leg). Just as his left foot nears the outside of your right ankle quickly bend your leg by bringing your right heel upwards behind you. Due to your evasive action your partner's left foot will pass harmlessly underneath your right knee. Immediately that you have succeeded in avoiding his left foot, progress by bringing your lower right leg forward and use the **sole** of your right foot to sweep against the inside of his right ankle. You should put this movement into effect as his left foot passes in front of your lower left leg, after having missed contacting with the outside of your right ankle. To aid your movements, incline your upper body to the right as you sweep against his inner right ankle bone and pull him in the same direction (Fig. 58). When his upper body is inclined more and more over to the left he will be forced to fall. You must glide him down on to his back and release your left hand from his right jacket sleeve, in order that he can break the fall with his right arm.

Do not make the mistake of raising your right foot in front of you, otherwise it would still be possible for your partner to throw you by forcing your foot upwards in between your legs. After practising the counter many times ask your partner to use his right foot against your left ankle, in order that you may counter him by sweeping against the inside of his left ankle with the **sole** of your left foot.

Countering a Stomach Throw

Grasp each other's jacket in the sleeve and lapel grip. Ask your partner to go through the motions of a Stomach Throw by bringing the sole of his right foot upwards towards your stomach. To start your counter measures relinquish the grip of your left hand from his right jacket sleeve, then step a small pace directly to your left with your left foot and follow this pace by taking a similar step in the same direction with your right foot. Now bring the palm of your left hand against the calf of his right leg and push his right foot past your right side. As soon as you cause his right foot to miss your stomach, push your right clenched hand firmly forward against the front of his left shoulder in the region of his collarbone. Step forward towards his right side on to your bent left leg, then bow forward from the waist and con-

FIG. 59

tinue pushing him over backwards with your right hand (Fig. 59). When he begins to fall backwards carry on adding power to your movements by bringing your head down towards the ground. Just before his back touches the mat he must let go of your right sleeve, so that he can break the mild fall with his left arm.

It very often happens in a contest that no point is awarded for this counter because an opponent invariably has time to sit down. Should this happen, however, it is still quite feasible to press home your attack by using a technique devised for use against an opponent in the supine position.

(TSUKURI)

THERE are three basic ways of closing with an opponent,
when most individual forward throwing actions are being
attempted from the standing position. It is best that each
different method is practised by you, in order that your
style becomes varied. I think it is unwise to claim that one
way is better than another, as each one, when performed
by an experienced man, is equally effective.

To avoid tedious explanations over the 'lefts and
rights', let us take it that all the preliminary movements
explained will culminate in the Sweeping Hip Throw
(page 54) against your partner's right side.

Withdrawing Left Foot
Start by holding one another's jacket in the sleeve and
lapel grip. Position your right foot slightly in advance
of your left foot. Now draw your partner's right arm
forward and slightly upward with your left hand and pull
his left jacket lapel towards the right side of your chest.
Immediately you put these actions into effect, withdraw
your left side by moving your left foot backwards in a
counter-clockwise movement and lodge your right elbow
underneath his left armpit. When you make this turn
pivot on the ball of your right foot to help your actions
and continue tilting your partner's upper body over the
toes of his right foot. After you have turned to face the
same direction as your partner plant your left foot on
the mat close to his left foot, with the toes of your foot
pointing slightly outwards (Fig. 60). Hold him firmly to
you by means of your hand grips on his jacket and transfer all the weight of your body on to your slightly bent left
leg. Raise your right leg outwards so that you can swing
it backwards against his right leg, making contact at the

front of his right thigh with the back of your right thigh and right buttock. When this reaping action is put into effect twist your hips to the left and keep your right foot pointing downwards to prevent your leg movement from being slowed down by tensed calf muscles. You should retain a hold on your partner's right jacket sleeve with your left hand as he begins to fall over your outstretched right leg. He should keep his grip on your left jacket lapel with his right hand and break the fall with his left arm. The main thing to bear in mind with this type of movement is that your right side is not moved forward until the throwing action is accomplished.

Advancing Left Foot
Begin by holding each other's jacket in the sleeve and lapel grip. Tilt your partner's upper body over the toes of his feet by drawing your hands towards you in the general direction of your ears. Step forward with your left leg and place the ball of your left foot on the mat in front of the toes of his left foot (Fig. 61). Now make a counter-clockwise turn by pivoting around on the ball of your left foot to your left and position your right elbow underneath his left armpit. When you begin pivoting your left foot to face the same direction as your partner, swing your right leg first outwards then inwards between your left leg and his legs and advance your right hip. Still maintaining the pulling actions of your hands, turn the toes of your left foot outwards as you complete your turning action and come to face the same direction to which

FIG. 60

FIG. 61

he is facing. Now bring the back of your right thigh into contact with the front of his right thigh, by swinging your right leg backwards in a pendulum-like movement with the foot turned downwards. When this action is put into effect, still maintain your pulls at his jacket and twist your hips to the left to ensure that you can bring him over your right leg to the mat. You should keep hold of his right jacket sleeve with your left hand, while he retains a grip on your left jacket lapel with his right hand. He must absorb the shock of his fall by striking the mat with his left arm.

Advancing Right Foot

Obtain the sleeve and lapel grip on each other's jacket, then tilt your partner's upper body over the toes of his right foot by drawing your hands towards your left ear. Move your right leg forward so that you can place the ball of your right foot on the mat just inside his right foot (Fig. 62). Now make a counter-clockwise turn to your left by pivoting around on the ball of your right foot and thrust your right elbow underneath his left armpit. After you have twisted round to face the same direction as your partner, plant your left foot on the mat just inside his left foot with the toes pointing outwards. Supporting the weight of your body on your slightly bent left leg raise your right foot outwards from the mat so that you can swing your right leg backwards against his

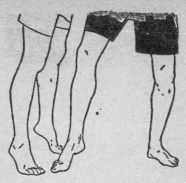

FIG. 62

right leg making contact at the thighs. As a result of these movements he will begin to fall over your right leg to the mat and you should twist your hips sharply to the left and continue pulling at his jacket to add power to your actions. He should break his fall by striking the mat with his left arm, while retaining a grip on your left jacket lapel with his right hand.

After you have gained a working knowledge of all three systems in respect of the Sweeping Hip Throw, look at the following techniques (which have been already explained) and adjust the feet movements where required, in order that you can use a different mode of approach for each individual throwing action: Shoulder Throw, Body Drop Throw, Sleeve Hip Throw and Basic Hip Throws.

11/ OBTAINING GRIPS ON AN OPPONENT'S JACKET

THERE are four basic ways of holding an opponent's jacket. These are termed in Judo as Sleeve and Lapel Grip, Armpit Grip, Sleeve Grip and Lapel Grip. Each method has its own particular advantages and disadvantages, and accordingly it would be unwise to claim that one is superior to the other. The important thing is that you make a real study of each type of hold in your efforts to gain an embracing style of Judo.

Sleeve and Lapel Grip
I feel that this grip is most suitable for beginners to use, as it tends to discourage the use of force, when the essentials of breaking an opponent's balance are being studied. The hold has the advantage of being neither solely defensive nor solely attacking (Fig. 63). The role of the left hand is to turn an opponent's body in a circular-like action, while the right hand is used either to draw an opponent into close contact, or alternatively hold him off should he try to achieve body contact. You will re-

FIG. 63

member that in the section dealing with Defence against Throwing Actions the 2nd Method concerned with Freeing an Arm was outlined for use against a smaller opponent who uses a Sleeve and Lapel Grip. Although this defence does not prevent the successful application of throwing movements such as Rear Throw, it does pose the largest obstacle to a person who favours the Sleeve and Lapel Grip. Another drawback with this type of grip is that it limits the number of techniques which can be performed against an opponent's left side.

Gripping Near the Armpits
This type of hold is the most widely used amongst advanced Judo exponents in Great Britain. The grip is taken on the opponent's jacket just by the front of his armpits (Fig. 64). Apart from being useful from the point of view of defence against throwing movements, it lends itself to throwing actions accomplished against either the right or left side of an opponent's body. Because of the quickness and ease with which one may vary an attacking movement, the lack of leverage due to the hands being somewhat close together is compensated by the element of surprise involved when suddenly changing the direction of attack.

Now that you have gained a fair knowledge of the Sleeve and Lapel Grip, I would recommend you to use

FIG. 64

the Armpit Grip and work through all the throwing actions once again, in order that you can use either a 'left or right side' technique.

Gripping the Jacket Sleeves
It is a rare occurrence to see this type of grip being used in Great Britain. Usually the hold is taken near the ends of an opponent's sleeves (Fig. 65). It could, I think, be termed as an 'all or nothing' grip, because it is of little use for a blocking form of defence, but is purely an attacking type of hold owing to the maximum amount of leverage it is possible to utilize. If an exponent is used to holding his opponent's jacket by the Armpit Grip, he usually favours throwing actions at close range; consequently, if you were to use the Sleeve Grip against him at the very onset of a contest or practice, before he has the opportunity to grip your jacket, he may be very disconcerted. This in turn may force

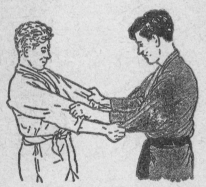

FIG. 65

him to grip your lower jacket sleeves and cause his timing to become affected by the unusual distances that you are apart. Should you be used to performing throwing movements at this range you would have the advantage. Probably the best throwing action it is possible to use in the Sleeve Grip is a Sleeve Hip Throw carried out against either the right or left side of the opponent. If you try to use this throwing action against an opponent's right side by raising his left arm with your right hand and he resists by forcing his left arm downwards, quickly reverse your movements by raising his right arm and accomplish a throwing action against his left side. Alternatively you can pull his left arm downwards with your right hand and carry out a throwing action against his right side when he forcefully resists by raising his left arm.

Gripping Both Lapels
This form of grip is purely defensive (Fig. 66). Due to the closeness of the hands and consequent lack of leverage, it is difficult to disrupt an opponent's balance without recourse to an excessive amount of strength. The main aim of the grip, plus a defensive crouch, is to force a

FIG. 66

draw. Sometimes in team contests one notices that a man, chosen for his defensive skill, uses this grip against the most skilled man of the opposing team who, it is considered, would score against any other team member and so adversely affect the result of the match. It is a defeatist attitude to adopt, but nevertheless it is a fairly common occurrence in Judo contests involving prestige. I do not recommend you to use this grip in practice.

(NE-WAZA)

THE technical term Groundwork is used to define the section of Judo devoted to techniques which are used from a lying or kneeling position. Apart from being a worth-while and essential branch of the art, Groundwork is perhaps more useful than throwing movements for increasing stamina and overall body fitness. This particularly applies to the sub-section of Immobilization Holds, and consequently if you use them on each occasion that you practise you will pave the way for becoming an expert at Judo.

General Defensive Tactics
Whenever you are lying on the mat on your back, you should bend your legs. If you lie with your legs outstretched it slows down your actions and renders you more vulnerable to attack. You will remember that it was explained earlier that immediately you fall or stumble to the ground, your feet should be brought nearest to an opponent to help in your defense if he attempts to follow you to the ground. On the supposition that an opponent will get inside the defensive screen of your feet you should aim to control him with your legs. If you manage to wrap your legs around his body it is practical to twist him over on to his back and so gain the advantage by taking up a kneeling position astride his chest. This can be achieved by pushing the sole of your left foot against his right knee and pulling at his jacket in the general direction of your left ear (Fig. 67).

Should you manage to wrap your legs around an opponent's body, but find it impossible to bring the sole of your foot against his knee due to his being too close to you, it is possible to use your legs to turn him on to

FIG. 67

his back. This can be brought about by swinging the inside part of your lower left leg against the outside of his right knee, and the inside of your right leg against his left hip (Fig. 68). When you put this scissor-like movement into operation you should turn on to your left side and pull the opponent in the same direction, so that you can turn him on to his back and kneel astride his chest.

If you are lying on your back and an opponent is kneeling close to your right side it may be difficult to ward him away with your feet, especially if he manages to step or kneel on the flaps of your jacket. Should you allow a wily opponent to get into such a position, the best way to frustrate him temporarily is to fully bend your right leg and right arm to bring them into contact with one another. The closer your right knee and right elbow are pressed together, the better your defensive screen will be (Fig. 69).

An opponent may stand by your feet and grasp your

FIG. 68

lower legs (or trousers) in an effort to swing your legs out at right angles to your upper body and so come to grips with you. If he tries to swing your legs to your left, position your right foot inside his lower right leg and cause the movement to be stopped. On the other hand, if he swings your legs to your right lodge your left foot inside his lower left leg. If you happen to be wearing long trousers, it is possible to break an opponent's grip on them by rotating the foot and lower leg around in a circular direction. After you have completed two circular movements it will have the effect of twisting an opponent's fingers and consequently make him release his hold.

Before reading further, I would recommend you to practise all four basic defensive methods diligently with your partner. Ask for his co-operation at first so that

FIG. 69

you may make quick progress and then reverse your roles in order that you can extend the same consideration to him.

General Attacking Tactics

If during a contest you cause an opponent to stumble or fall, without the conditions of a point resulting, you are able to follow up your attacking movements by using a Groundwork technique. Should he attempt to frustrate your aim by using his feet to ward you off, grip his ankles (or trousers) and swing his legs first to the left and then to the right. When you swing his legs to your right let go and step forward to his right side. To avoid his blocking your advance by positioning his bent right leg between your upper bodies, you should quickly place your lower right leg against his right side.

Should an opponent succeed in impeding your advance by lodging a foot between your legs as explained in the defensive tactics, you are able to vary your movements and so overcome this form of defence. This is achieved by gripping his legs (or trousers) at the knees and stand-

ing by the outside of his right leg. Once you have succeeded in pressing his legs against the ground walk forward and gently place your right knee on to the right
side of his chest.

If you are in a kneeling position between an opponent's
legs, do not ever try to apply a lock or hold against him
until you have escaped from in between his legs. One
way to achieve this aim is to bring your right hand be-

FIG. 70

tween your body and his left thigh, and by sliding it
underneath his thigh obtain a tight grip on the left side
of his belt or jacket, while grasping the right side of his
jacket with your left hand. Once this hold is taken you
can escape by using the crook of your right arm to turn
the opponent over on to his right side by bringing his
left leg over your head (Fig. 70). Care must be taken
to see that his leg passes very close to the top of your
head, as otherwise he will be able to bend his leg and
position it in front of your chest.

Another way of escaping from in between an opponent's legs is to pinion one of his legs on to the mat. If
you are kneeling between his legs grip his left thigh or
trouser leg close to the inside of his left knee and force
the outside of his left thigh against the mat. To add power

to your movements bring your right knee quickly forward and press it on to the inside of his left thigh (Fig. 71). When you succeed in doing this it is a simple matter to clamber over his thigh to his left side and come to grips with his upper body.

FIG. 71

During a contest it sometimes happens that an opponent stumbles forward on to his hands and knees. Should he feel that he has no time to rectify his exposed position, he may well adopt a purely defensive posture by gripping his alternate jacket lapels tightly with his hands and tucking his chin well down on to his chest. If you strive to break up this defence by trying to pull him over, or tugging at his arms, you will probably not succeed. The essential thing to accomplish at first is to turn him on to his back. Do this by bending your legs and standing close to his right side. Your right hand should be used to grip his right jacket sleeve while your left hand should grasp his right ankle (or trouser leg). To twist him on to his back **snatch** at his sleeve and lower right leg as you straighten your legs (Fig. 72). As soon as his back contacts the mat you should drop your right knee quickly, but gently, on to his chest to stop him rolling over again into his original defensive position. When practising this with your partner it is best for him to break the fall with his right arm, as a powerful twisting action results in quite a heavy fall. As a matter of interest I believe that

FIG. 72

fishermen of the West Indies use a similar movement to turn huge turtles on to their backs by gripping the edge of their shells! If you are opposed by a fairly experienced opponent it sometimes proves worth while to incline your upper body over him and use your hands to grip his left sleeve and left ankle (or trouser leg). By doing this you will be able to twist him over on to his back by pulling him towards you, while stepping quickly backwards. This would catch him unawares; especially if he is set to resist your efforts to twist him away from you. When you practise this variation your partner should break the fall with his left arm.

As I recommended after the few defensive tactics were explained, it is best if you practise with your partner before reading further.

(OSAEKOMI-WAZA)

IMMOBILIZATION HOLD is a term used in Judo to describe a method of holding an opponent on the mat so that the greater part of his back rests against the surface and the movement of one or both of his arms is restricted. It is the finest section of Judo for developing stamina and for giving exercise to all the muscles of the body. For this reason the technique of holding ought to be practised by all aspiring Judo exponents, even though they do not appear spectacular when compared with the other sections of the art.

The important principle to bear in mind with regard to Immobilization Holds is that they should be applied by using the weight of your body. Although it is necessary to tense your arm muscles in order to achieve a firm grip on an opponent's jacket it is not expedient to tense other groups of muscles. Very often the greatest obstacle met with by beginners when practising Immobilization Holds is that they tense the muscles of their arms easily enough, but unfortunately the other muscles of the body also become tensed. One way of putting it would be to say that a beginner's body is like a solid bar of iron, whereas a fairly experienced exponent has iron-like arms but a jelly-like body. Now, as we know, even if the two commodities were of equal weight it would be far easier to lift 'the iron bar' than 'the jelly'. In effect the bar of iron acts as one solid unit, but the jelly behaves as several units. This then is the idea. When you apply a hold against your partner imagine that your body is disjointed and jelly-like to such a degree that if he succeeds in affecting one part, the other parts will still remain slumped on him or the mat. With the practical application of this idea it is quite possible to hold a man who under favourable circumstances could lift double the weight of your body or even more. In this connec-

117

tion a Weight-Training Instructor, who is an acquaintance of mine, was watching our Judo class practising Immobilization Holds and mentioned that he thought it easy for a strong man to break a hold applied by a physically smaller man, irrespective of considerations such as skill. I knew this man to be capable of lifting quite fantastic iron weights and in the interests of experimentation I asked him to allow me to apply an Immobilization Hold against him, to see if he could escape. Although he did succeed in lifting me bodily in the air for a second or two at a time, he could not hurl me from him and after some fifteen minutes' fruitless struggling he was forced to admit that he could not escape from the hold.

You should practise the holds which are outlined together with your partner, but remember to request his co-operation in the early phases of training.

It is forbidden by the rules to push against an opponent's face when trying to escape from a hold, or to use any form of blows; nonetheless, it is quite permissible to use all of your strength and skill in your efforts to escape.

1st Hold. Variation of Upper Four Quarters (Kami-shiho-gatame)

Ask your partner to lie down on the mat on his back and then take up a kneeling position by the right side of his head. Incline your upper body over him and grip the left side of his belt or jacket with your left hand, then grasp the right side of his belt with your right hand. Tuck your elbows into his armpits to restrict his movements to a certain extent and outstretch your legs behind you, so that you can press your stomach against the mat close to his right shoulder (Fig. 73). Press your chest against his chest and make sure that your legs are kept well apart in order that you make it difficult for him to turn you over on to your back. If he tries to free himself from your hold by arching his body on his feet and shoulders (or head) you should press the toes of your feet firmly against the mat and hold your head back. He may also try to create a gap between your body and his by moving quickly round in a circular direction. You should counter this by following his movements, taking great

FIG. 73

care that your legs are not brought too close together. To avoid making this mistake, practise moving one leg, say six inches, and then move the other one the same distance, to ensure that your knees are never less than shoulder width apart. Do not try to hold your partner's body in the same place on the mat, but move with him and use your upper body to pinion his back to the ground.

Interchange roles with your partner in order that you both become suitably fast in applying the hold.

2nd Hold. Variation of Side Four Quarters
(Yoko-shiho-gatame)

Request your partner to lie down with his back resting on the mat, while you take up a kneeling position by his right hip. Slide your right hand in between his thighs and then underneath his left thigh, until you are able to grasp the left side of his belt or jacket. Your left hand should be passed underneath his left shoulder, until you can clasp the left side of his jacket close to his left armpit. Outstretch your legs behind you and drop your stomach on to the mat close to his right hip. Tighten your grips on his belt and jacket by hugging him close to you and keep your feet well apart (Fig. 74). In this hold your body should be at right angles to your partner's. If the angle is much less than a right angle, that means to say your feet are near his, he may be able to catch your right leg with his lower right leg and so escape.

FIG. 74

On the other hand if he tries to turn towards you on to his right side, press your toes against the mat and arch your back by pressing your head and shoulders back. Should he try to turn on to his left side hug him firmly to you with your hands and drop your upper body firmly on to the right side of his chest.

It should be noted that this hold is vulnerable to a neck lock.

3rd Hold. Variation Scarf Hold (Kesa-gatame)

Your partner should lie down on the mat and allow you to stand facing him by his right side. Recline to the ground on to your right buttock close to his right side. Pass your right hand over his body and then slide it underneath his left armpit. Now you are able to grasp the back of his collar at the nape of his neck with your right hand by bringing your fingers over the palm of your hand. Continue your movements by gripping his upper right jacket sleeve with your left hand and trap his right lower arm under your left armpit by clamping your left elbow against your left side. Make sure that his left arm is kept bent, otherwise he may be able to free his arm too easily. Your feet should describe the hands of a clock when showing eight o'clock, the right foot being the min-

FIG. 75

ute hand, your left foot being the four hand (Fig. 75).
Your legs should be bent in such a way that your right
foot, left knee and left heel are in alignment with one
another. In your efforts to control your partner's struggles drop the weight of your upper body on to the right
side of his chest and draw his collar underneath his back.

If your partner attempts to roll you over his body by
turning on to his right side and gripping you around the
waist with his left arm, you must keep the muscles of
your body relaxed even though he might succeed in lifting you partially from the ground. Should he try to move
away from you in an effort to create a gap between your
right hips, counter his efforts by moving your legs and
body to follow his movements. Reverse the instructions
where necessary and perform the same hold against his
left side.

4th Hold. Variation Shoulder Hold (Kata-gatame)

Your partner should lie down on his back, while you sit
down on the mat close to the right side of his chest.
Pass your right hand over his chest and then slide it
underneath the nape of his neck. Now bend your right
leg and grasp the inside of your own right thigh with
your right hand. Your partner's head should now be
encompassed by your bent right arm. Clasp the outside
of his upper right arm with your left hand and push his
arm forcibly to your right. Continue by lowering your

FIG. 76

head until your right ear is positioned close to the back of your left hand. His right arm should be forced against the right side of his neck by the continuous pressure of your left hand (Fig. 76). Your feet and legs should be almost in the same relative positions as the hold immediately preceding this one. Care must be taken to see that your head is kept close to the mat, as otherwise your partner could clasp his hands together and use his right elbow effectively to force you away from him. Provided you keep your head close to the ground and hold him tightly his right arm will be deprived of three-quarters of its potential strength.

5th 'Hold'
Although this hold and the following one do not fulfil the conditions of a recognized Immobilization Hold, I have decided to include them, nonetheless, because of their usefulness for learning how to control a struggling opponent.

Ask your partner to sit down on the mat and allow you to sit on the ground behind his back. Pass your

FIG. 77

hands forward underneath his respective armpits and grip his jacket lapels tightly with both hands. Recline backwards to the mat, then wrap your legs around his body and hook your lower legs inside his respective thighs. In order to control him properly, draw his jacket lapels towards his armpits and thus further restrict his movements (Fig. 77). When your partner attempts to free himself, move with him and make every effort to keep behind him, even if he succeeds in rolling over. His aim should be to escape from the hold of your legs and hands by twisting and turning as much as possible.

6th 'Hold'
Request your partner to lie down on the mat and then kneel down close to his right hip. Lower your upper body on to his chest and place your lower arms on the mat close to the left side of his body. Now outstretch your legs behind you and keep your feet about one yard apart. Your elbows should be kept lodged against the left

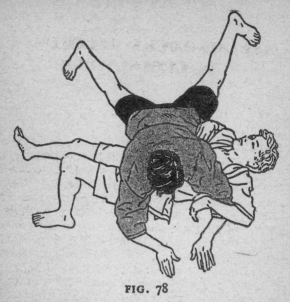

FIG. 78

side of his body (Fig. 78). Drop your stomach on to the mat close to his right side and move with your partner as he struggles to free himself. Your forearms should be used to stop your partner from escaping from under you by moving them to the left or right. You can also grip his jacket with your hands if you wish.

14 / ARMLOCKS APPLIED IN GROUNDWORK

(UDEGATAME)

IN JUDO the term 'Armlock' is used to define a way of applying contrary pressure against an opponent's arm which causes the elbow joint to lock (and less often the shoulder joint). It should be clearly understood that no armlock can be successfully brought into play without a sound knowledge of the basic essentials of methods of holding. In effect one is complementary to the other. It is unwise to concentrate exclusively on the locks, with little thought given to the essential preliminary movements which pave the way for their application. This is one reason why you should spare no effort in acquiring a good working knowledge of Immobilization Holds. This does not mean, however, that you need rely on Holds for gaining points in Groundwork. Indeed, if you are not very heavy it is best to use armlocks for scoring, as body weight does not play such a large part in their application. By this I do not claim that Holds cannot work against a heavier man, merely that there is little point in concentrating on all of his upper body when one or both of his arms are handy!

The most important rule to remember in all armlocks applied against a straight arm is that pressure against an opponent's wrist is always exerted in the opposite direction to that of his thumb. Before reading further, fully extend your left arm, then spread your fingers and move your thumb round in a circular direction. You will have noticed that provided your arm was fully extended the movement of your thumb directly affected your left elbow joint. This then is the principle to work on. By looking at an opponent's thumb one is able to tell exactly in what direction his wrist must be moved in order to bring about a locking of his elbow joint.

In the case of armlocks applied against a bent arm the basic essential to remember is that an opponent's hand should be kept close to the relative side of his body as the lock is applied. This will ensure that the leverage at the disposal of his arm is drastically limited, thus paving the way for a successful lock. If, as you start to apply an armlock, an opponent is able to react by tensing his arm muscles or putting up any other form of strong resistance, you must transfer your attention to his other arm. It is a bad principle to try using **force** to bring about any lock. Apart from the slowing down process which always results, you may well cause an opponent an unintentional injury. This is because you may suddenly overcome his resistance and not be able to stop your powerful movements in time to avoid hurting him. Conversely, should you be the defender (at a later stage in your training), do not try to resist while a particular lock is being applied, but offer a spirited counter attack by using a different technique against him, **before** he has a chance to bring his lock into play.

Unfortunately in Judo a defensively minded opponent sometimes avoids armlocks from being applied by a skilled opponent, by crossing his wrists and holding his alternate jacket lapels. Although this would not mean that you would be brought to a standstill if you quickly modify your actions, it is the equivalent of engaging in a practice bout of boxing with an opponent who takes care not to advance closer than six yards to you, lest you are able to touch him with a glove. Bearing in mind that Judo is a competitive sport, I urge you not to use this and other artifices in an effort to bring about stalemate.

Before going into the few armlocks which are given, you should make sure that you both agree to certain rules. Your partner *must submit immediately* any discomfort is felt, by tapping your body twice with his free hand, or by calling out 'stop'. In the early stages of practice you must apply the locks both gently and in slow motion, until with the passing of time you can judge the exact pressure needed for their successful application. You may come up against little difficulties at first with these armlocks, but provided you help one another the minor problems will gradually become resolved. In an effort to clarify things I have given the exact positions at the time of application. Remember: **Do not use any force whatsoever in practice.**

1st Armlock

This type of armlock is expedient to use after you have thrown an opponent to the ground without gaining a point, due to the lightness of his fall. You should throw your partner to the mat with one of the throwing actions explained previously and retain a grip on his upper right jacket sleeve with your left hand. Stand close by the right side of his upper body and bend over him as soon as he breaks the fall with his left arm. Tug at his right jacket sleeve with your left hand in order that his arm becomes straight and he is forced on to his left side. Continue your movements by passing your right hand underneath his right upper arm and gripping your own left wrist. Clamp your right elbow against your right side to trap his right wrist underneath your right armpit. The thumb edge of your right wrist should be pressing against the back of his right elbow. Once your right arm is positioned correctly, relinquish the grip of your left hand from his jacket sleeve and press the palm of your hand securely against the front of his right shoulder (Fig. 79).

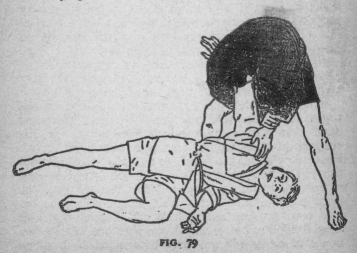

FIG. 79

To apply the armlock press your left hand firmly against
his right shoulder and bring your right wrist **slowly** upwards against the back of his elbow joint. It is essential that your partner's right arm be kept straight
and contrary pressure applied against his arm, as otherwise the armlock is made ineffective.

2nd Armlock

This armlock is most usefully employed when you have
succeeded in applying the 3rd Hold on page 121 and an
opponent puts up such a struggle that he manages to free
his right arm from the grip of your left hand. Alternatively you may use a little cunning and purposely let an
opponent free his right arm, in order to gain a quick
point by using this armlock.

Ask your partner to disengage his right arm from the

FIG. 80

grip of your left hand and arm. Once he does this grasp his right wrist with your left hand, then push his forearm downwards, thus enabling you to raise your left knee from the mat and clamp the inside of your left thigh over the thumb edge of his right wrist. Bring your right knee close to his right shoulder by bending your leg (Fig. 80). At this stage the tension on his right arm should be increased by nipping it between your thighs. To apply the lock use the contrary pressure of your legs against his arm. This is achieved by lowering your left knee and thigh to the ground, while slightly raising your right knee and thigh. Your partner must submit directly he feels the slightest discomfort, by tapping your right arm twice with his left hand, or by calling out 'stop'. The most common mistake which beginners make when applying this lock is to relax the pressure of their right side against the right side of the opponent's chest, and by doing so allow him to raise his body to ease the tension on his arm.

3rd Armlock

Request your partner to allow you to apply the 3rd Hold as described on page 121. On this occasion you should not call on him to free his right arm from the grip of your left hand, but take the initiative and apply an armlock against him. Grasp his upper right jacket sleeve as tightly as possible with your left hand and keep his right forearm trapped under your left armpit. Now lean slightly backwards and slide your right foot forward beyond the right side of his face. This movement will enable you to swing your left leg in a forward clockwise movement and lodge your left calf against the left side of his neck. At the time that you make this movement, twist your upper body slightly to the right and face your partner, thus making the movement of your left leg much easier (Fig. 81). To apply the armlock press your stomach *slowly* forward against his right elbow joint and push downwards against his right wrist by lowering your left shoulder. In effect this movement entails the arching of your back. Once again your partner should submit without delay.

Practise swinging your lower left leg in a forward circular direction over your partner's head many times,

FIG. 81

until you become adroit at lodging the calf of your leg against the left side of his neck. A usual fault made by a beginner in the application of this armlock is that an opponent's arm is not held tightly against the side of the body. Consequently, when the lock is about to be applied it is found that the opponent has been allowed to slide his right wrist out from underneath the left armpit and so nullify the pressure against his arm.

4th Armlock

This is another armlock which follows on from the 3rd Hold which was outlined on page 121. In this illustration let us suppose that you have managed to apply the hold against your partner, but in this instance he does not try to free his right arm in an effort to escape your hold. Request your partner to slide the thumb of his left hand inside the left side of your collar just below your left ear, in such a way that the little finger edge of his left wrist is nearest to your throat. You should begin your counter movements by sliding the fingers of your left hand between his left wrist and your throat until you are able to place the palm of your hand against your left cheek. This movement will make it impossible for him to press his wrist against your throat and pave

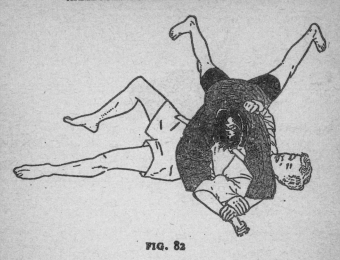

FIG. 82

the way for you to gain absolute mastery over his actions. Continue your counter measures by pressing the little finger edge of your left wrist against the inside of his left wrist and force his arm down towards the mat just by his left side. On putting this action into effect turn on to your front by bringing your right leg backwards underneath your left leg. As soon as you turn face downwards, press your chest on to his chest and spread your legs wide apart so that your body is at right angles to his. Now slide your right hand underneath his upper left arm and grasp your own left wrist (Fig. 82). To apply a bent armlock against him pull his left wrist **slowly** inwards with your left hand and twist the knuckles of your right hand forward and then downwards towards the ground, in order to achieve a twisting action of your left wrist. A mistake which numerous beginners make when practising this lock is to allow the opponent's arm to be situated above the line of his shoulders and thus afford his arm to have too much leverage at its disposal.

5th Armlock
Your partner should lie down on the mat on his back and allow you to kneel astride his chest. Ask him to push

against your right shoulder with his left hand. As soon as he does this action grasp his left wrist tightly with both hands in an alternate thumb grip, ascertaining that your thumbs press against the pulse side of his wrist. Pull his wrist forward and upwards to such an extent that his left arm becomes perfectly straight, then incline your upper body slightly to your left. Now bring your right knee off the mat and swing your lower right leg in a forward anti-clockwise direction over his head, until you are able to place the sole of your right foot on the mat close to his right ear. At this stage your right calf should be pressed against the front of his throat and the outside part of his upper arm should be held firmly against the inside of your right thigh by means of your grips on his left wrist (Fig. 83). To apply the lock at this juncture pull his left wrist to your right, ensuring that his thumb points to your left, and make certain that your upper right leg is used to apply a contrary pressure on his arm, by pressing inwards against his limb in the region of his elbow joint.

In a contest it is sometimes necessary to stabilize your balance when you are faced by an opponent of no mean skill. To prepare for such an occasion practise the following combination movement with your partner.

Let us take it that you have succeeded in applying a

FIG. 83

lock on your partner's left arm as just described. Relax
your grips on his left wrist, in order that the tension
on his arm becomes eased, and gently recline to the mat
on to your right side. Take care to notice that the outside of your right ankle is placed across his throat
throughout this movement to deter him from sitting up
(Fig. 84). To apply the lock from this position tighten
your hold on his left wrist once again then pull it downwards and raise your knee so that the inside of your
right thigh presses upwards against his left elbow. Twist
his wrist if necessary to ensure that the thumb of his
left hand is uppermost and you are able to apply the
pressure correctly. A mistake to avoid when applying the
lock in this position is that of reclining to the mat too
far away from your partner's left side and consequently
affording his left arm more scope for movement. You
should reverse the instructions where necessary so that
you can apply a lock against his right arm.

6th Armlock
This armlock can be used as an alternative to the one

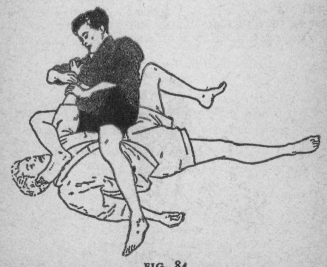

FIG. 84

just given. Ask your partner to lie down on the mat on
his back and kneel astride his chest. Request him to push
his left hand forward against the right side of your chest.
As soon as he pushes his left hand against your chest
grip his left wrist tightly with both hands in an alternate
thumb grip, in order that your thumbs press against the
pulse side of his wrist. Slide your left foot forward
beyond his right shoulder, then bring your right leg forward beyond his right shoulder, then bring your right leg
forward in an anti-clockwise circular movement, until you
are able to lodge your right calf underneath the right
side of his face or chin. On performing this movement
you should pull at his left wrist in order that his arm
becomes straight and recline to the mat on to your left
side. By the successful application of these actions your
partner should be lying on his right side. The inside of
your right thigh ought to be pressed down against his
left arm in the region of his elbow joint (Fig. 85). To
apply an armlock against him ensure that you keep the
thumb of his left hand nearest the mat as you raise his

FIG. 85

left wrist and press **gently** downwards against the back of his elbow with the inside part of your right thigh.

Your partner should help you in the initial stages by rolling over on to his right side. You must both be very careful at first as this is another very powerful lock. After you have gained a working knowledge of applying the lock against his left arm change the instructions where necessary and apply the lock against his right arm.

7th Armlock

This is another armlock which can be successfully brought into play when you are kneeling astride your partner's chest. On this occasion ask your partner to grip your throat as though he intended to pull you forward and attempt a stranglehold. You should grasp his jacket sleeves with your hands and bring your knees forward until you are able to clamp the inside of your thighs firmly against his upper arms. Still retaining your grips on his jacket sleeves, bow forward from the waist so that you are facing him. At this point his arms should be completely straight, with the outside of his upper arms

FIG. 86

and shoulders firmly held between your thighs. Transfer your grips from his sleeves to his wrists and slowly pull his wrists outwards with both hands while pressing inwards against his upper arms with the inside part of your thighs (Fig. 86). These final movements will cause both of his arms to become locked and he must submit immediately any discomfort is felt, by striking the mat two or three times with the soles of his feet or by calling out 'stop'. Due to the position of your partner's arms, he will be able to utilize a fraction of their normal strength, so be very careful to see that only a little pressure is exerted against his wrists. The most usual mistake made by a beginner in this armlock is to allow his knees to move outwards when pulling at an opponent's wrists. Provided that the person applying the lock keeps his knees clamped tightly against an opponent's upper arms, two fingers are enough to use against an average person's arms to bring about the lock.

8th Armlock

Ask your partner to lie down on his back and then take up a kneeling position astride his chest. Request him to bend his left arm and position it by the left side of his face. Keeping your left hand palm downwards, tightly grasp his left wrist and incline your upper body forward over him. Slide your right hand underneath his left upper arm and grip your own left wrist. At this point the thumb of your left hand should press against the pulse side of his left wrist and the thumb of your right hand should press against your left wrist in a similar way (Fig. 87). Twist his left wrist inwards and downwards by twisting the knuckles of your right hand forward and downwards, while still retaining a grip on your left wrist.

Practise the movements over and over again, until you become used to applying the lock while your partner's arm is resting against the mat: then ask him to raise his bent left arm from the ground and practise grasping his left wrist with your left hand in mid-air, before pushing his arm **gently** back to the surface and applying the final movements necessary to create the lock. It should be noted that the closer his left elbow is brought to his left hip, the stronger the armlock becomes. After you

FIG. 87

have become adept at applying the lock against his left arm, practise applying it on his right arm before changing places with him.

15 / TWENTY COMMON MISTAKES TO AVOID IN JUDO

ALTHOUGH I have pointed out certain basic errors which students tend to make when learning Judo, I think it worth while to itemize twenty of the more common mistakes.

1. Refusing to help a partner in the early stages of practice and consequently making every technique difficult for him to learn.
2. Using strength before the basic skills are acquired.
3. Trying to overcome an opponent's resistance by using a greater amount of strength.
4. Keeping the legs well bent when moving around the mat and so slowing down the speed of your movement.
5. Keeping your arm muscles continuously tensed in an effort to balk an opponent's throwing actions.
6. Staring down at an opponent's feet, which in turn causes your upper body to be inclined forward.
7. Gripping an opponent's jacket too tightly before trying a throwing action.
8. Kicking an opponent's ankle with the inside bone edge of your foot when trying Sweeping Ankle Throws, instead of using the sole of your foot.
9. Bringing your feet close together when moving round the mat and so giving an opponent an easy opportunity to throw you.
10. Staying in the same relative position for longer than is necessary after an opponent has checked or avoided your initial attacking movement.
11. Thinking about what throwing action you will use against an opponent before a practice or contest has started.
12. Attempting to block a heavier opponent's throwing actions, rather than avoiding them and using a counter-throwing technique.

138

13. Bending forward from the waist when trying to throw an opponent, without pulling his upper body in the same direction.

14. Holding on to an opponent's jacket with both hands due to a misguided sense of pride when he has succeeded in throwing you.

15. Leaning over an opponent who is lying on the ground (after being properly thrown by you) instead of keeping a good sense of balance by bending your legs and holding your head back.

16. Allowing an opponent who has thrown you to stand over you as you regain your feet.

17. Turning your back to an opponent when getting up after being thrown, or when engaged in Groundwork.

18. Lying down on the ground with your legs outstretched rather than limiting the scope of an opponent's attack by keeping them bent.

19. Attempting to come to grips with an opponent on the ground who has succeeded in wrapping his legs around your body, instead of escaping from in between his legs first.

20. Tensing all the muscles of your body in a mistaken effort to increase the power of an Immobilization Hold.

16 / METHODS OF PRACTISING JUDO

AFTER you have worked through all the techniques in this book, I recommend you to practise competitively with your partner. This stage should be arrived at after you have co-operated with one another for two months. Should you have the opportunity to practise with others, so much the better. There are three basic ways used in Judo for improving one's skill, which are as follows:

Standing Practice (Uchikomi *or* Butsukari)
This way of improving skill takes the form of trying throwing action against an opponent without his moving about the mat or attempting evasive action. The object is to improve your movements as well as the power of your throwing actions. Your opponent is permitted to use 'blocking tactics' but not to counter you with a throwing technique. You for your part should tell him what technique you intend to use and not try to catch him unawares by suddenly using a variation. Once you succeed in lifting his feet from the mat, do not make the mistake of throwing him to the ground; it only wastes time and effort.

Many Judo exponents use this type of training when they wish to improve their skill at a particular technique.

Free Practice (Randori)
This is the most widely used system for improving skill and fighting ability. The aim is to move about the mat together with an opponent and to use your efforts to score against each other. In most Judo clubs after a student has progressed to Yellow Belt this type of practice forms the bulk of his training. The objects are to improve the co-ordination of movement and give the opportunity for improvement of fighting ability. It would not be an exaggeration to claim that this form of training is the finest

yet devised for improving the ability of a Judo exponent.

Usually a free practice with a particular opponent should not last for more than ten minutes, before another opponent is invited to a test of skill. The more opponents you practise with the more variable are the styles you will encounter. You will find that the greatest obstacle at the beginning is the difficulty of applying techniques on the move, as it were.

Contest (Shiai)

This is the most competitive form that Judo takes and the idea is to use all of your energies against an opponent. There is a distinction drawn between this style and 'free practice'.

Contests are only held for grading examinations and between teams; consequently I do not think it advisable for you to practise this strong style of Judo until a much later stage in your training.

Due to the fact that Japanese terms are used by Judo
exponents of many nations, I have given them with their
English equivalents where possible. The following glossary
is by no means exhaustive, but it will suffice for a basic
knowledge. I have hyphenated the Japanese words where
practical for facilitating pronunciation.

THROWING TECHNIQUES

Ashi-guruma	Leg Wheel Throw
Deashi-harai	Advancing Ankle Throw
Hane-goshi	Spring Hip Throw
Hane-makikomi	Spring Winding Throw
Harai-goshi	Sweeping Hip Throw
Hiza-guruma	Knee Wheel Throw
Ogoshi	Hip Throw
Oguruma	Leg Wheel Throw
Okuri-ashi-harai	Sweeping Ankle Throw
Osoto-gake	Outer Hook Throw
Osoto-gari	Rear Throw
Ouchi-gari	Inner Ankle Throw
Seoi-nage	Shoulder Throw
Sumi-gaeshi	Corner Throw
Tai-toshi	Body Drop Throw
Tanio-toshi	Valley Drop Throw
Tomoe-nage	Stomach Throw
Tsuri-komi-ashi	Drawing Ankle Throw
Tsuri-komi-goshi	Sleeve Hip Throw
Uchi-mata	Inner Thigh Throw
Uki-goshi	Floating Hip Throw
Yoko-guruma	Side Body Throw
Ashi-gatame	Armlock by using a leg
Gyakujui	Reverse Cross Neck Lock
Gyakujujimie	Reversed Half Cross Neck Lock

Hadakajime	Choke Neck Lock
Hiza-gatame	Armlock by using knee
Kami-shihi-gatame	Upper Four Quarters Hold-down
Kataiujijome	Half Cross Neck Lock
Kesa-gatame	Sitting Thigh Hold-down
Namijuji	Normal Cross Neck Lock
Okurieri	Stranglehold from behind
Ude-garami	Bent Arm Lock
Ude-gatame	Armlock
Yoko-shiho-gatame	Side Four Quarters Hold-down

**N.B.—Strangleholds have not been described in this book
because of their dangerous potentialities unless practised
under the personal supervision of a qualified Black Belt.**

GENERAL TERMS

Atemi—Blows. Taught only to exponents of Black Belt
grade.

Butsukari—Standing Practice. Used for improving a
particular throwing technique.

Dan—Black Belt. The teaching grade.

Dojo—Practice Hall. The place where Judo is practised.

Hajime—Referee's permission to start a contest.

Hidari Shizen-tai—Left Natural Posture. Left foot slightly in advance of right foot.

Hiki-wake—Drawn Contest. Signified by Referee crossing his arms at wrists.

Ippon—Point. Referee awards a point to a contestant
(*see* Contest Rules).

Jigo-tai—Defensive Posture. Adopting a crouching posture in an effort to force a draw.

Judo—The way of overcoming an opponent, by appear-
ing to give way.

Judogi—Outfit. Costume worn when practising Judo.

Judoka—Judo Man. One who is a student of Judo.

Ju-jutsu—The ancient form of Judo.

Kaeshi-waza—Counter technique.

Kuzushi—Breaking balance. Disturbing an opponent's
balance.

Kyu—The student grades up to and including Brown
Belt.

Migi Shizen-tai—Right Natural Posture. Right foot slightly in advance of left foot.

Nage-waza—Throwing techniques.

Ne-waza—Groundwork. Techniques applied from a kneeling or lying-down position.

Randori—Free Practice. A competitive, free-moving test of skill.

Shiai—Contest. The most competitive form that Judo takes.

Shizen-tai—The normal upright posture.

Tatami—Mat. A mat composed of straw; also fibre or rubber.

Tsukuri—Positioning. Preparatory movements leading into a technique.

Waza—Technique. Any Judo movement applied against an opponent.

Waza-ari—Half point. Awarded by a Referee for a mild form of throwing action.

Yuseigachi—Referee's decision. Award of a drawn contest to one of participants who has shown best style.